THIS IS THE WAY
IT WORKS

THIS IS THE WAY IT WORKS

A COLLECTION OF MACHINES
BY ROBERT GARDNER

Illustrated by Jeffrey Brown

DOUBLEDAY & COMPANY, INC.
GARDEN CITY, NEW YORK

Library of Congress Cataloging in Publication Data

Gardner, Robert, 1929-
    This is the way it works.

    Includes index.
    SUMMARY: Explains the mechanisms of such machines
as the iron lung, the incandescent light bulb, a zipper,
and a roller coaster.
    1. Machinery—Juvenile literature. 2. Electric
apparatus and appliances—Juvenile literature.
3. Medical instruments and apparatus—Juvenile literature. [1. Machinery] I. Brown, Jeffrey, 1948-
II. Title.
TJ147.G37   680   79-7493

CONTENTS

MEDICINE AND HEALTH

RECREATION

IN THE FUTURE

LIGHT

As early as 1802, Sir Humphry Davy, an English chemist, found that metal strips would glow when an electric current passed through them. He also noticed that the hot metal burned away rather quickly as it combined with the oxygen in the air. In 1879, Joseph W. Swan, in England, and Thomas A. Edison, in the United States, independently developed practical incandescent light bulbs by sealing carbon filaments in evacuated glass bulbs.

INCANDESCENT LIGHT BULB

The carbon filament used in Edison's first light bulb could not be heated to high temperatures without seriously reducing the lifetime of the bulb. Since the light emitted by a filament increases with temperature, researchers in the late 1800s began searching for materials that would withstand high temperatures so that brighter bulbs could be manufactured.

By 1909, engineers had devised a method for drawing tungsten metal into very fine wires, as thin as 1/100 millimeter. Tungsten has a very high melting point (3382°C or 6145°F) so it can be heated to 3000°C, at which point it is white hot. Unfortunately, these thin tungsten wire filaments evaporated slowly at such high temperatures, coating the bulbs with a thin black film and then falling apart.

To reduce evaporation, inert gases such as nitrogen and argon were added to the bulbs. While these gases increased the service life of the tungsten filaments, it was found that they formed convection currents inside the bulbs. The moving currents of gas carried heat away from the filament, reducing its temperature and, therefore, the brightness of bulbs. Later it was discovered that convection currents could be reduced and high temperatures obtained by winding the filament into a fine coil.

The filament in a modern bulb (*see diagram*) is supported by several molybdenum wires. The ends of these wires are imbedded in a glass button at the top of the button rod. The copper and nickel lead-in wires that

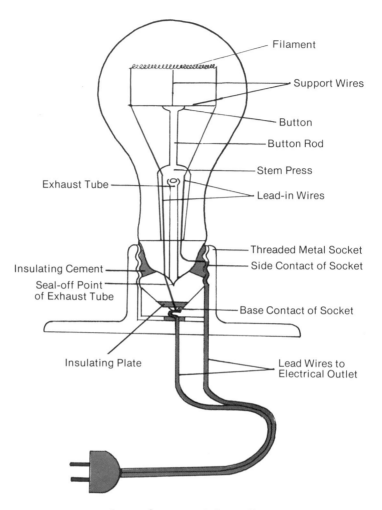

Filament

Support Wires

Button

Button Rod

Stem Press

Exhaust Tube

Lead-in Wires

Threaded Metal Socket

Insulating Cement

Side Contact of Socket

Seal-off Point
of Exhaust Tube

Base Contact of Socket

Insulating Plate

Lead Wires to
Electrical Outlet

Incandescent Light Bulb

connect to opposite ends of the filament are supported by the glass stem press through which they pass. One lead-in wire is soldered to the metal plate at the very end of the base; the other wire is connected to the side of the threaded metal base. There is no electrical connection between these contact points because they are separated by the insulating plate. Electric current can enter either lead-in wire, pass through the filament, and exit through the other lead-in wire.

The exhaust tube leads from the stem press to the base of the glass bulb. During the manufacturing process the bulb is evacuated through this tube and the bulb is flushed with nitrogen and argon gases to remove any oxygen that might be trapped inside. The bulb is then partially evacuated and the lower end of the exhaust tube heated until the glass around it melts, sealing the bulb from the outside air. Finally, the lead-in wires are soldered to their contacts and the glass bulb cemented to the threaded metal base.

Unplug a lamp so there is no danger of your getting a shock. Remove the bulb and look at the interior of the lamp socket. You will see where the light bulb contacts touch the contacts in the socket.

Common light bulbs are manufactured in various sizes from 15 to 150 watts. The wattage is determined by multiplying the current that passes through the bulb by the voltage across the bulb. The voltage across all types of bulbs and most appliances is about 120 volts. Consequently, it is really the current flowing through the bulb that determines the wattage. The filament in a 15-watt bulb is only about 0.014 millimeter thick. Such a thin wire offers a lot of resistance to the flow of electricity. A current of only about 1/8 ampere flows through the bulb's filament. The filament in a 30-watt bulb is slightly thicker, allowing a 1/4-ampere current to flow through the bulb. What current do you think flows through the filament of a 60-watt bulb? . . . a 120-watt bulb?

Most Christmas-tree lights do not have the same shape as ordinary bulbs and, of course, they are usually made from colored glass. However, if you take one apart, you'll find that the inside resembles a small incandescent light bulb. But what about blinking Christmas-tree lights? What makes them go on and off?

BLINKING CHRISTMAS-TREE LIGHTS

Use a magnifying glass to look at the inside of a blinking Christmas-tree light bulb. You will find that it resembles the bulb shown in *diagram A*. Instead of two lead-in wires that connect with opposite ends of the filament as in ordinary incandescent bulbs, there are three wires. Wire 1 is a lead-in wire. It is firmly attached to one end of the filament. Wire 2 is connected to the other end of the filament but, as you can see, it ends in the glass bead. This wire is not the other lead-in wire—wire 3 is. Notice how wire 3 is bent so that it touches wire 2. Why does the bulb have three wires?

Wire 3 is made by soldering together two different metals such as iron and brass to form what is called a bimetallic strip. Like all metals, brass and iron expand when heated and contract when cooled. However, brass expands or contracts about twice as much as an equal length of iron when the temperature changes. This means that a bimetallic strip must bend when heated or cooled (*diagrams B and C*).

To see why the strip bends, put both your elbows on a table and place the palms of your hands together in front of your face. Now, pretend that your two arms are a bimetallic strip. Your left arm is brass and your right arm is iron. If a bimetallic strip is heated, the brass will get longer than the iron. Imagine that your left or "brass" arm is getting longer than your "iron" arm. Since you can't make your left arm grow, slowly raise your left elbow to make believe that the "brass" arm is lengthening. You will find that your "bimetallic" arms move to the right.

When electricity flows through the filament of the blinking bulb, the wires get hot. Wire 3, the bimetallic strip, bends away from wire 2 as it warms and the circuit opens. This prevents electric current from flowing between wires 2 and 3. With no current, the wires cease to glow and quickly cool. The cooling bimetallic strip (wire 3) bends back and touches

12

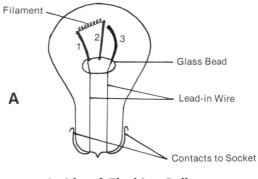

Inside of Flashing Bulb

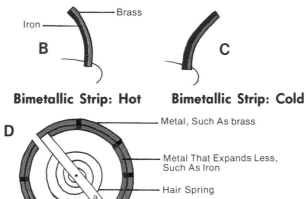

Bimetallic Strip: Hot　　　**Bimetallic Strip: Cold**

Balance Wheel

wire 2 again, current flows, the light goes on, the wires get hot, wire 3 bends away, the circuit opens, and on it goes, blinking away until the circuit is disconnected.

Bimetallic strips were not invented to make lights blink, nor are they used only at Christmas time. You can probably figure out how they are used in automatic thermostats that turn on heating systems when a room or a house gets cold, in fire alarms, in some dial thermometers, and in coffee makers. They are even used in the balance wheels of a watch. The metallic arm, a (*diagram D*), in a balance wheel lengthens if the temperature rises. This would make the watch run slower. To counteract the increased length of the arm, the bimetallic strips attached to the ends of the arm bend inward. Consequently, the wheel turns at the same speed for all temperatures.

Watch for bimetallic strips. You'll find them in many different kinds of machines.

Only about 10 percent of the energy from an incandescent bulb is in the form of light. In an energy-conscious world, it is not surprising that cooler, more efficient, fluorescent lamps have become the major source of electric lighting in the United States. A 40-watt fluorescent bulb gives about six times as much light and lasts about five times longer than an incandescent bulb of the same power.

FLUORESCENT LAMP

A fluorescent lamp is similar to a neon sign. Both are gas discharge tubes, but the gas in a fluorescent bulb is mercury vapor and the tube is coated on the inside with a fluorescent powder called a phosphor. When ultraviolet light strikes the inside walls of the tube, the fluorescent powder emits visible white light. But where does the ultraviolet light come from?

Many fluorescent lamps have starters in them. When you turn on the light, several seconds pass before the tube emits continuous light. This time delay is due to the starter, which is used to establish an electric current along the tube. The starter contains a glow lamp and a bimetallic strip. The voltage across the glow lamp is enough to ionize (form charged atoms and electrons) the gas in the lamp and thereby produce a small current across the lamp. The current warms the bimetallic strip, which bends, bringing the two contacts together. This forms a short circuit across the glow lamp.

Because current no longer flows across the glow lamp, it goes out and a large current is now established around the circuit that includes the cathode wires of the fluorescent tube. As these wires get hot, the bimetallic strip cools, because very little heat is produced there now that current can flow through the cathode wires.

As the bimetallic strip bends back to its original position, the circuit opens suddenly and current stops flowing. The rapid drop in current through the ballast sets up a changing magnetic field that produces a high-voltage "kick" large enough to produce an arc of current between the hot cathodes. Once this arc is established, all the current flows through the tube. The voltage across the glow lamp is now too small to send any current across the lamp.

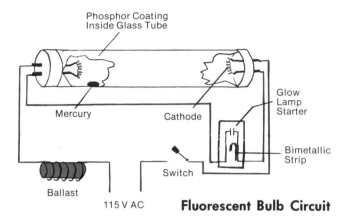

Phosphor Coating Inside Glass Tube

Mercury

Cathode

Glow Lamp Starter

Bimetallic Strip

Ballast

Switch

115 V AC

Fluorescent Bulb Circuit

Current Through Glow Lamp Heats Bimetallic Strip

Hot Bimetallic Strip Short Circuits Glow Lamp

The electric current through the tube consists of electrons that are "boiled" off the cathodes. As they move across the evacuated tube, many of them collide with mercury atoms that have vaporized as the cathodes released heat. The mercury atoms absorb energy from the fast-moving electrons. The electrons within these "excited" atoms of mercury are raised to higher energy levels. This means that they circle the nucleus at a greater distance. When these electrons "fall" back to lower energy levels, they emit yellow, green, blue, violet, and ultraviolet light.

The ultraviolet light is absorbed by the chemicals in the fluorescent coating that then release the absorbed energy as visible light (a mixture of all the colors in the rainbow).

The lighting delay and flicker found in lamps with starters has been eliminated in more recent fluorescent lights. Instant-start lights have a

16

transformer that produces a high voltage across the cathodes so that an arc is produced immediately. Rapid-start lights contain special cathodes that heat quickly and establish an arc at lower voltage.

Because the light from various fluorescent chemicals differs, it is possible to make fluorescent tubes that emit more or less warm and cool colors. Such types of tubes as warm white, cool white, white, deluxe warm white, deluxe cool white, daylight white, and even plant-growth tubes rich in the colors absorbed by plants are available. Cool, warm, and daylight whites give the maximum amount of light per watt of power. The deluxe tubes are designed to emphasize certain colors that they illuminate. Both deluxe and plant-growth tubes produce about 30 percent less light per watt than standard tubes.

Centuries before Christ, Egyptians, Greeks, and Romans had learned to make mirrors by polishing metals. Coated glass mirrors were made by Venetian craftsmen in the sixteenth century. They made a "sandwich" by pouring mercury on a sheet of tinfoil and then covering the mercury with paper. A sheet of glass was slowly lowered onto the paper, which was withdrawn, bringing the bottom surface of the glass into contact with the mercury. The mercury and tin combined to produce a reflecting surface that adhered to the glass.

In 1835, Justus von Liebig discovered that a solution of formaldehyde, ammonia, and silver nitrate, when heated, would deposit a fine layer of silver metal on glass. This method, called silvering, is similar to the process used today to make common mirrors. More expensive mirrors are produced by heating a metal such as aluminum in a vacuum chamber. The metal vapor condenses on a glass plate to form a thin reflective layer.

MIRRORS

Mirrors are everywhere—on cars, trucks and motor bikes, in bathrooms, parlors, hotel lobbies, handbags, amusement-park fun houses, and telescopes. You can find them in unexpected places, too, on the surface of a calm pond or puddle, in a window at night, even in your soup spoon.

When you look into a plane (flat) mirror, your image appears to be behind the mirror and looks just like you. However, if you are right-handed, your image will be left-handed. With concave mirrors, your image will be larger than you when you are close to the mirror and upside down when you are far from the mirror. Convex mirrors, such as those found in stores and on the sides of trucks, always form images that are smaller than the objects.

To understand how mirrors work, you must first know that light travels in straight lines. Then you must know what happens to light when it strikes a mirror or any very smooth surface. You can find out by placing a mirror on a narrow beam of light, commonly called a ray of light. The light entering a dark room along a door that is slightly opened makes a

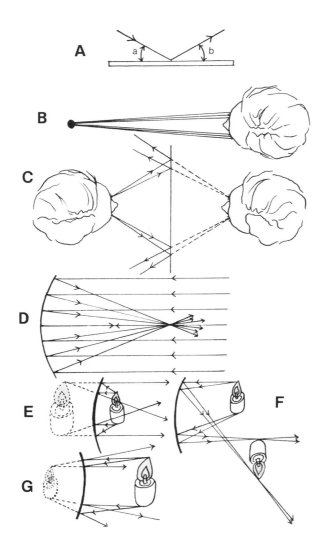

A. Reflected Ray of Light, B. Diverging Rays, C. Mirror Image, D. Focal Point of Curved Mirror, E. Virtual Image, F. Real Image, G. Virtual Image

satisfactory beam or ray. As you can see from *diagram A*, the angle between the narrow light beam and the mirror is the same before and after reflection (angle a is equal to angle b). This is true for all angles and, as you will see, allows us to explain why mirrors form images.

Diagram B illustrates how we locate objects in space. Our brains automatically estimate the divergence (spreading) of the light rays coming from an object to our eyes. The point where these rays come from is the position of the object as we see it.

When light rays from an object bounce off a mirror, they do so as shown in *diagram A*. But there are an infinite number of light rays from each point on an object. Each ray strikes the mirror at a slightly different angle and so each ray is reflected at a slightly different angle. From *diagram C*, you can see that the reflected rays from any point on an object seem to come from or meet at a point behind the mirror. In fact, if you draw these rays carefully with a ruler and protractor, you will see that they come from a point that is as far behind the mirror as the object is in front of the mirror.

What you see in the diagram for two points of light, one from from each eye, is true for every point on the object. The image is a point-for-point reproduction of the object. You should also notice that the image is turned around right for left; that is, the image's right eye is made from reflected light that came from the object's left eye. The man parts his hair on the right side, but the image parts his on the left.

Of course, there is not actually anything behind the mirror. The image only appears to be there because that's where the light rays seem to be coming from. For this reason such images are called *virtual* images.

A concave mirror, such as a shaving mirror, obeys the same law of reflection, but the reflecting surface is curved like the inside of a dish. Such a mirror will bring parallel rays of light together at a point in front of the mirror. This point, called the *focal point*, is shown in *diagram D*.

If a light source is placed at the focal point of a concave mirror, the light rays will be reflected as a parallel beam of light. As you might guess, concave mirrors are used to make spotlights and automobile headlights.

Such mirrors are also used for shaving or applying makeup. An object placed between the focal point and the mirror will produce an enlarged image as shown in *diagram E*.

Diagram F shows what happens if something is placed beyond the focal point. The image is now found in front of the mirror. It is upside down and it is a *real* image, not a virtual image. It is real because the light rays really do come together to form an image; they do not merely *seem* to come from the position of the image. You can convince yourself that such images are real by holding a sheet of paper or cardboard in front of a concave mirror that is reflecting light from some distant object such as a light bulb on the other side of the room. Move the paper back and forth until you get a nice sharp image. Remember, the image will be upside down, but as you can see, it is real.

As well as serving decorative purposes, convex mirrors are used in stores to help detect shoplifters and on trucks to observe following traffic because they reflect a larger field of view than a plane mirror. From *diagram G*, you can see that the images formed in convex mirrors will always be virtual and smaller than their corresponding objects.

Now that you know how mirrors work, see if you can figure out why you can see so much more in a plane mirror when you are close to it than when you are far away from it. Can you also explain why the field of view seen in a convex mirror is so much wider than the field seen in a plane mirror?

Since its invention by Zacharias Janssen in 1590, the microscope has been an indispensable tool for biologists. Similarly, the telescope has played a major role in astronomy for centuries.

MAGNIFIERS AND MICROSCOPES

When light passes from air to glass or water, it suddenly changes direction. Put a pencil in a glass of water. You will see that it appears to bend at the point where it enters the water. Place a coin in a teacup. Lower your head so that the coin just disappears below the edge of the cup. If someone slowly adds water to the cup, the coin will reappear. Light from the coin that would not normally reach your eyes is bent when it leaves the water, enabling you to see it (*diagram A*).

When parallel rays of light pass through a convex lens (a magnifying glass), they are brought together at a point called the focal point (*diagram B*). The distance between the lens and the focal point is called the focal length of the lens. The focal length depends on the curvature of the lens. Fat lenses have a short focal length, while thin lenses have a long focal length. If an object is placed between the lens and the focal point, light rays from the object are bent as they enter and leave the lens, producing a virtual image that is larger than the object (*diagram C*). The magnification is greatest when the object is just a little inside the focal point.

If the object is placed beyond the focal point, the lens will form a real image (*diagram D*).

A microscope has two convex lenses with very short focal lengths (less than 5 centimeters). The specimen to be magnified is placed just beyond the focal point of the objective lens (*diagram E*) so that a large real image of the object is formed. The eyepiece lens is used to magnify this real image. The image that you see through the eyepiece is a virtual image of the real image formed by the objective lens. It may be as much as 1,000 times larger than the specimen being examined. The image is also reversed so that when you move the specimen to the right and down, the image moves to the left and up. This is why it takes practice to use a microscope well.

A refracting telescope like a microscope is made from two convex lenses. Because the object under investigation is normally very far away,

22

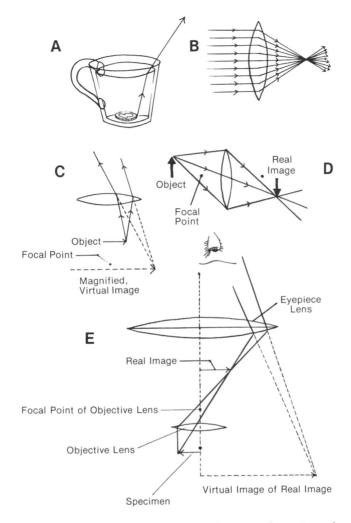

A. Refracted Ray, B. Lens Brings Light Together, C. Enlarged Virtual Image, D. Real Image, E. Images in a Microscope.

the focal length of the objective lens is usually 30 centimeters (1 foot) or more in order to make the image as large as possible.

To collect enough light to make the image bright, the objective lens should be wide. The distance across the lens is called the aperture. The largest aperture for a refracting telescope is 100 centimeters. However, lighter reflecting telescopes that use concave mirrors to gather light can have very large apertures. The reflecting telescope at Mount Palomar has a diameter of 500 centimeters (200 inches). Long-exposure photographs taken with this telescope show that there are 5,000 galaxies in a 1° square of the sky. The sun's diameter covers about 1/2° of sky, so in one day the sun passes in front of nearly 1,000,000 galaxies as it crosses the sky.

The distance across a galaxy varies, but an average distance is about 30,000 light years. A light year is the distance light travels in one year—5,878,000,000,000 miles (9,370,000,000,000 kilometers). The distance across a galaxy then is about 176,000,000,000,000,000 miles (280,000,-000,000,000,000 kilometers). Of course, we can't begin to imagine such distances, but it does help us to appreciate the vastness of the universe.

The slide projector had its origin in the magic lantern—*a favorite form of entertainment in the nineteenth century. Scenes or figures that had been painted on a piece of plane glass were projected in enlarged form onto a screen or wall by holding a flickering candle just behind the glass.*

PROJECTORS: SLIDE, MOVIE, OPAQUE

You can build a simple slide projector of your own by setting up the materials shown in the first diagram. The second diagram shows the major parts of a slide projector you might find in your home or school.

An incandescent lamp with a coiled filament serves as the light source. The major purpose of the light is to illuminate the slide, of course. It is placed at the center of curvature of a concave mirror so that light that would normally escape through the rear of the projector is reflected back through the filament of the light source. This nearly doubles the intensity of the light that illuminates the slide. Before passing through the slide, the light enters a condenser (a set of convex lenses) that concentrates the light and produces an image of the filament in the tube containing the projection lens. This prevents such an unwanted image from appearing on the screen.

Some light passing through the transparent colored or black-and-white slide is scattered in all directions. The projection lens gathers light from the slide to form a real image on a screen.

This lens can be moved back and forth so that the image may be focused clearly on a screen. This is usually accomplished by mounting the lens in such a way that it can be moved by a system of gears controlled by a single knob. If the screen is moved farther from the projector, the distance between the slide and the lens must be decreased.

In some projectors a plate of special heat-absorbing glass is placed inside the condenser so that the slide will not melt from the high temperature generated by the intense light. A fan is often included within the machine to help remove heat.

A movie projector is similar to a slide projector. It is a bit more complicated because twenty-four stationary frames (separate pictures) are projected every second. The film has holes along the side so that a *claw* with points on it can pull each frame into the *gate* where light from the

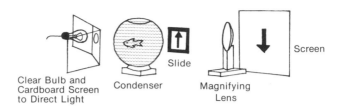

Clear Bulb and
Cardboard Screen
to Direct Light

Condenser

Slide

Magnifying
Lens

Screen

A Homemade Projector

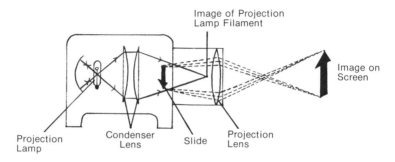

Image of Projection
Lamp Filament

Image on
Screen

Projection
Lamp

Condenser
Lens

Slide

Projection
Lens

Slide Projector

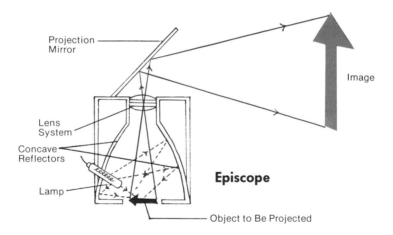

Projection
Mirror

Image

Lens
System

Concave
Reflectors

Episcope

Lamp

Object to Be Projected

condenser shines through the transparent frame. When one frame is replaced by another, a rotating shutter covers the gate.

Images persist on the retinas of your eyes for a few hundredths of a
second, so we are not aware of one picture or frame replacing another.

26

Instead, we see the series of pictures as if we were observing normal motion.

An episcope or opaque projector (shown in the third diagram) is used to project flat pictures or diagrams such as those found in books. Concave mirrors within the episcope increase the amount of light that falls on the object to be projected. A mirror at an angle of 45° above the projection lens reflects the rays bent by the lens to form an image on a screen. If the mirror were not there, where would you see the image?

We normally associate light with heat. After all, incandescent bulbs are hot, fire is hot, and the sun, if we could go there, would surely be hot. But now scientists have discovered a cold source of light, and have invented packages that suddenly emit light when bent.

COLD LIGHT

You bend what looks to be a slim plastic rod. Suddenly an eerie yellow-green light, about as bright as a candle, fills and surrounds the plastic tube. Yet the rod, which you now guess to be a magic wand, remains cool and can be held in your hand. It continues to glow for hours.

What is the source of this cold light? It is surely not a fluorescent bulb, because it has no electric connections and is colder than any fluorescent lamp you have ever known.

The plastic tube that you bent contained a liquid and a thin-walled glass ampule filled with a second liquid. Bending the tube broke the ampule

"Excited Molecule."

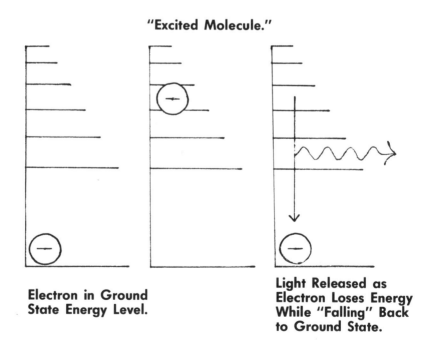

Electron in Ground State Energy Level.

Light Released as Electron Loses Energy While "Falling" Back to Ground State.

28

inside, allowing the second liquid to mix and react with the other fluid. The product of this reaction is a *chemiluminescent* substance. The molecules of this substance were "excited" during the reaction. This means that electrons within the molecules were raised to higher than normal energy levels. When the electrons "fall" back to the normal ground state level, the stored energy is released as light (*see diagram*).

The chemicals in the wand produced a yellow-green light but other colors are produced by different chemiluminescent substances.

These tubes are not used primarily as magic wands. They serve as emergency light sources in planes or cars and, particularly, around explosive materials where open flames or electrical sparks would be dangerous. They are used as markers for pilots who have had to parachute into the sea, and for camping, fishing, boating, and other activities.

A similar cold light is being developed for use in homes. It consists of a liquid and a pair of metal electrodes in a sealed glass tube. When the electrodes are connected to a source of electricity, the liquid chemical decomposes at the electrodes and then recombines between the electrodes, emitting light as it does. The process is still inefficient, but researchers believe that it will eventually be more efficient than fluorescent lighting.

As early as 1917, Albert Einstein showed that according to theory, it should be possible to stimulate atoms of an element to release stored energy as coherent light. But it was not until 1954 that Charles Townes and Arthur Schawlow were able to produce a coherent beam of microwaves. Their device was called a maser, short for Microwave Amplification by Stimulated Emission of Radiation. In 1958, Townes's calculations predicted the possibility of producing a coherent beam of light by similar means. Theo Maiman discovered a way to do this, using a ruby crystal in 1960. The device became known as the laser (Light Amplification by Stimulated Emission of Radiation). Since that time a number of materials other than rubies have been used to make lasers.

LASER

An atom of any element has a positively charged nucleus that is surrounded by an equal negative charge in the form of electrons (*see diagram A*).

When atoms are heated or bombarded with light or fast-moving electrons, they may absorb energy and become "excited." As atoms absorb energy an electron or electrons within the atom are raised to higher energy levels; that is, they move farther from the nucleus (*see diagram B*). After a short time these electrons lose energy and "fall" back to lower energy levels. The energy lost by the excited atoms appears as light.

If a large number of electrons in different atoms all "fall" from energy level 3 to energy level 1, a lot of light will be emitted. All this light will have the same wavelength. If electrons fall from level 4 to level 1, the energy released will be greater and the light emitted will have a shorter wavelength. Light with more energy has a shorter wavelength. The wavelength of the light emitted when electrons fall from level 2 to level 1 will be longer than that released when the electrons fall from level 3 or 4 to level 1.

In all cases, light is released in the form of tiny bundles of energy called *photons*.

The atoms in the crystal of a ruby laser, for example, are excited by a

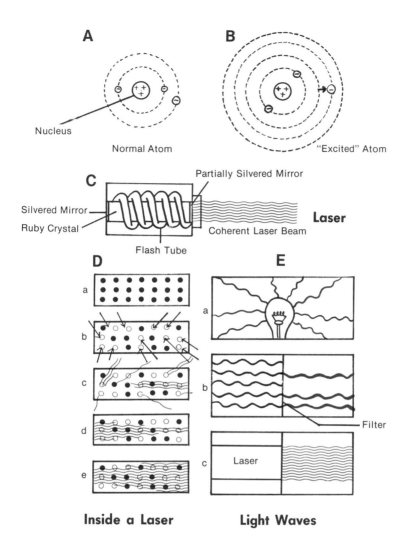

A

Nucleus

Normal Atom

B

"Excited" Atom

C

Partially Silvered Mirror

Silvered Mirror

Ruby Crystal

Flash Tube

Coherent Laser Beam

Laser

D

a
b
c
d
e

E

a
b
c

Filter

Laser

Inside a Laser　　　**Light Waves**

flash tube that surrounds the crystal rod (*diagram C*). The green light emitted by the flash tube "pumps" electrons in the chromium atoms of the ruby crystal to high energy levels (*diagram D*). These electrons quickly fall to an intermediate energy level and then, more slowly, to their original "unexcited" level. As this final energy drop occurs, a photon of red light is released. When this photon passes by another excited atom, it stimulates the atom to emit its own red photon as it falls back to its original energy level. These two photons now stimulate two more atoms to release photons, and so on until a huge number of identical photons fill the crystal.

Many photons escape from the sides of the ruby crystal, but those that move along its axis are reflected by the silvered mirror at one end of the laser and the partially silvered mirror at the other end. As the light is reflected back and forth, more and more atoms are stimulated to emit the same red photons. Finally, after a few millionths of a second, a pulse of red light bursts through the partially silvered mirror and the "pumping" process begins again.

Because the pulses occur again and again every few millionths of a second, we see a continuous beam of light emerging from the laser.

The light from the laser is *coherent*. Ordinary light, such as that from a light bulb, is incoherent. It contains a great variety of wavelengths and the light spreads out in all directions as it leaves the bulb (*diagram E*). If a very good colored filter is placed over the light, all the light coming through the filter may have the same wavelength, but it will still not be coherent. The waves will not be in phase; that is, they will not be "in step" (*diagram b*). The laser light is in phase and all the wavelengths are identical (*diagram c*). Because it is coherent, the beam does not spread out as it travels away from the laser.

The straight parallel rays of light in a laser make it an ideal instrument for surveying or measuring large distances. Laser beams bounced off the moon have been used to measure the earth–moon distance very accurately. A lens can be used to focus a powerful laser beam to a point. The intense heat at the focal point can be used to weld metals. Less intense laser-beam energy may be used to "weld" a detached retina to its eyeball.

Lasers are also used to make three-dimensional pictures called holograms, to transmit and store vast amounts of information in very little space, and to induce the atoms in tiny pellets of frozen hydrogen to fuse, forming helium while releasing large quantities of energy. Scientists and engineers are trying to find a way to contain and use the energy released by this laser-induced fusion of hydrogen. If they succeed, we will have an almost unlimited source of energy.

APPLIANCES

According to legend, goats introduced humans to coffee during the ninth century when Kaldi, an Abyssinian goat-herder, decided to try a few of the berries that his goats seemed to find so tasty and invigorating. Kaldi, in turn, introduced the berries to a Moslem monk, who spread the word.

By the time the first European coffeehouse opened in London in 1652, people had learned to make a beverage by using hot water to extract the chemicals from the coffee beans.

COFFEE MAKERS

The odor of freshly made coffee in the morning is surely as American as apple pie and far more common. But how do coffee makers work?

An increasingly popular coffee maker is shown in *diagram A*. To make it work, you simply place ground coffee in a paper filter, pour cold water in the top of the machine, press the switch, and wait several minutes.

While you wait, electricity flowing through the heating coils raises the temperature of the bimetallic strip at the bottom of the water pan. The strip bends slightly so water can flow slowly onto the hot drip plate, over the heater, and through the hole at the center of the heating element to the coffee in the filter below.

The bimetallic strip is designed to bend just enough to let about 5 milliliters (1/6 ounce) of water pass through the hole in the bottom of the pan each second. The heater can supply the heat needed to bring this much water to very nearly the boiling point in about one second. Therefore, the water that falls onto the ground coffee is very hot even though the water remaining in the top pan is still cold.

The hot water seeps through the coffee-filled filter into the pot at the base of the machine. After the top pan has emptied, the main heating coil is turned off and the smaller hot plate turned on to keep the coffee warm.

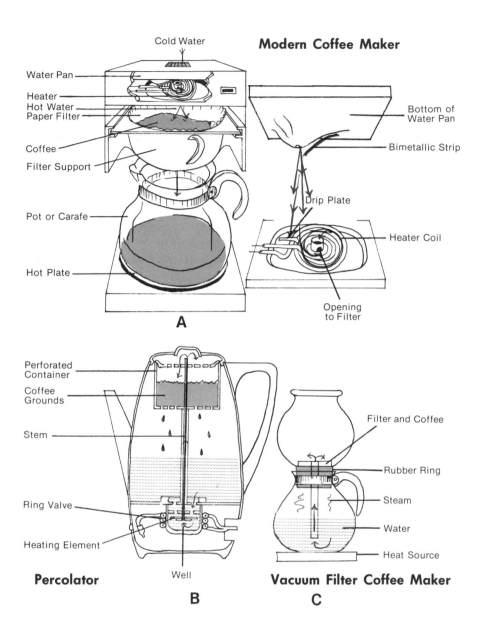

Cold Water

Modern Coffee Maker

Water Pan

Heater
Hot Water
Paper Filter

Coffee

Filter Support

Pot or Carafe

Hot Plate

Bottom of
Water Pan

Bimetallic Strip

Drip Plate

Heater Coil

Opening
to Filter

A

Perforated
Container

Coffee
Grounds

Stem

Ring Valve

Heating Element

Filter and Coffee

Rubber Ring

Steam

Water

Heat Source

Percolator   Well   **Vacuum Filter Coffee Maker**

B   **C**

A percolater-type coffee maker also heats only small quantities of water at one time. Water flows into the well and stem (*diagram B*) through an opening just above a ring-shaped valve. The brewing (heating) element quickly brings the small quantity of water to a boil. Increased pressure due to the steam bubbles produced closes the valve and forces the small amount of hot water up the stem. Water emerging from the top of the stem is deflected downward to a porous cover that spreads it over the coffee grounds in the perforated container. After flowing through the ground coffee, the liquid brew falls back into the pot where it mixes with the cold water and can be pumped up the stem.

Once steam and hot water leave the stem, the pressure in the well decreases, the ring valve falls, and another small amount of water enters the well to be heated.

A thermostatic switch turns off the current to the brewing element when the liquid in the pot reaches the proper temperature. The same device then sends electricity to a separate warming element that keeps the coffee hot.

Many restaurants and diners use vacuum-filter coffee makers. Cold water is placed in the bottom container or pot. The second container which has a long tube extending from its base is placed on the pot. A rubber ring between the two containers forms an airtight seal. Ground coffee is poured over the filter at the base of the upper chamber, and the coffee maker is placed on a stove or hot plate.

As the coffee maker is heated, steam is formed. The pressure above the water increases and forces the hot water up the tube and out over the ground coffee.

After the hot water has been in contact with the coffee grounds for a while, the heat is turned off. The steam in the lower container condenses. This reduces the pressure in the pot or, as some say, it creates a partial vacuum. The air pressure above the water in the upper container is now greater than the pressure in the pot, and the liquid coffee is pushed down into the lower container. The upper container is then removed so coffee can be poured from the pot.

The strength of the coffee can be controlled by the length of time the liquid is heated. As long as steam is produced in the pot. pressure will keep the bulk of the liquid in contact with the coffee grounds above the filter.

For those who are not coffee connoisseurs, there is a much simpler method. Place a teaspoonful of instant coffee in a cup, add hot water, and stir.

Clothes hanging from a line used to be a common sight, but today clothes driers probably outnumber clotheslines. While the average annual energy required to operate a drier is about 1,000 kilowatt-hours, it is an extremely useful machine. Even energy-conscious people appreciate its value during rainy periods or the short cold days of winter.

CLOTHES DRIER

What makes clothes dry fast when they hang on a line? Try some experiments of your own and you'll find that dry air (low humidity), warm air, moving air (wind), and maximum exposure of the wet surface all increase the rate at which water evaporates from wet clothes.

A clothes drier is designed to do all the things that you know make clothes dry fast. The air entering the drier is warmed by electric heating coils or a gas flame. The heating coils can't take water out of the air to reduce the humidity, but warm air can hold or dissolve, if you will, much more water vapor than cold air. Warming the air then has the same effect as using dry air—it can hold more moisture. The rotating drum bounces and spreads the clothes, exposing more surface to the warm air. The air is circulated through the drier by a fan. This has the same effect as hanging the clothes in a mild breeze.

The diagrams illustrate how all this is done. When you turn on the switch, electricity flows through a set of heating coils (or a gas heater is ignited) and an electric motor begins to rotate. The motor turns both the big hollow drum that contains the wet clothes and the fan that drives moist air out the exhaust pipe. As air leaves the drier, the pressure within the rotating drum decreases. This causes fresh air to flow in through the intake vent where it passes over the heating coils before entering the spinning drum.

As the warm air flows over and through the tumbling clothes, it becomes saturated with water vapor before passing through the exhaust duct, fan, and exhaust pipe. The entrance to the exhaust duct is covered with a removable lint trap to remove particles that might clog the ducts.

After the time clock is started, bimetallic thermostats, similar to those found in coffee makers or heating systems, control the temperature within

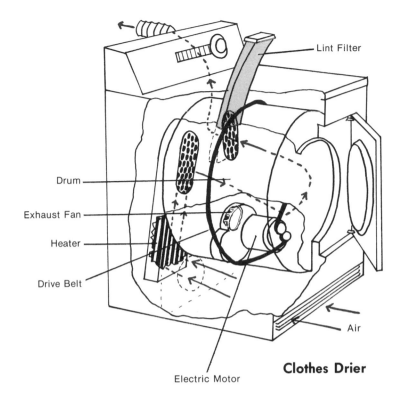

Clothes Drier

Lint Filter

Drum

Exhaust Fan

Heater

Drive Belt

Air

Electric Motor

the drum. The heat absorbed by the evaporating water keeps the temperature down until the clothes are nearly dry. As the temperature rises above about 57°C (135°F), the thermostat opens the heater circuit and the timer turns off the motor a little later.

The warm dry clothes can then be removed and stored without ever stepping outside.

Each year a family of four must wash 30,000–40,000 items such as glasses, plates, cups, silverware, pots, and pans. An automatic dishwasher makes this task a lot easier. It does use more energy (350 kilowatt-hours per year), but only half as much as a refrigerator (730 kilowat-hours), and 30 percent of that used by a frost-free refrigerator (1,200 kilowatt-hours).

AUTOMATIC DISHWASHER

When you turn on an automatic dishwasher, you hear water entering the machine. Later you hear some sloshing, turning, splashing, and pumping. This happens several times. During the quiet period that follows, you will find the appliance is quite warm. Once the light goes out, you can open the dishwasher door and find a load of warm clean dishes.

The switch used to start a dishwasher is a timer that turns valves, motors, and circuits on and off in proper sequence.

The first event in the sequence is the opening of the inlet valve that allows hot water to enter the tub. Normally, the timer turns the valve off when the water reaches the proper level, but most dishwashers have a float valve that will stop the water flow should the inlet valve fail to close.

Once the tub is filled and the inlet valve closed, the timer establishes electrical contact between the motor and the power source. The motor begins turning in a direction that causes the upper impeller to pump water through the spray arms. These arms rotate as water rushes from their small openings for the same reason that a balloon zips about a room when air rushes out its neck. The water is pushed slightly sideways by the arms as it emerges from the openings. The water in turn pushes back against the arms and so they rotate, spraying water all over the dishes. As the five or so gallons of water are circulated through the pump and spray arms at a rate of about fifty gallons per minute, the water mixes thoroughly with the detergent or soap that was added just before closing the door. The hot moving solution removes or dissolves any small food particles that remain on the surface of the dishes.

The timer turns off the motor for a few seconds to let the dishes drain. It then starts the motor spinning again but in the opposite direction, so that the lower impeller now pumps water out of the tub.

40

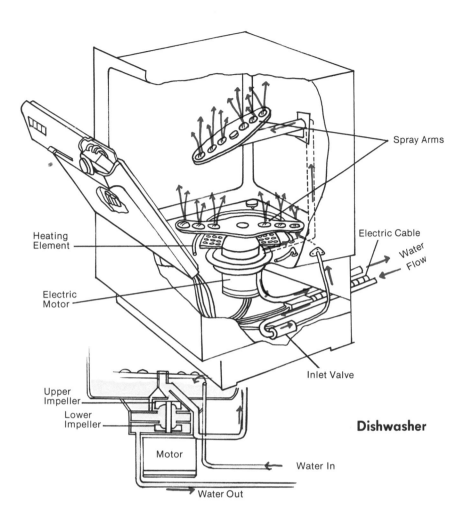

Dishwasher

Labels on diagram: Spray Arms, Heating Element, Electric Motor, Electric Cable, Water Flow, Inlet Valve, Upper Impeller, Lower Impeller, Motor, Water In, Water Out

After the soapy water has been pumped through the drain hose or pipe, the cycle is repeated. This time hot water rinses any remaining soap or detergent from the dishes.

Finally, the timer sends electricity to the heating element that lies below the lower tray of dishes. The temperature of the air within the dishwasher rises to about 82°C (180°F). The air vent opens, allowing the warm moist air to escape. This increases the rate at which water evaporates from the dishes and so speeds the drying process.

The dishes may now be removed for another eating cycle.

Since the dishwasher uses about one kilowatt-hour of electricity each time it operates, it is not economical to use the appliance unless it is filled with dishes. Therefore, unless you're a member of a large family, you will probably not turn on the machine more than once a day.

There is an enormous variation in the wavelength of electromagnetic waves. Radio waves are about 100 meters long while gamma rays have a wavelength of only 10^{-14} meters (0.00000000000001m); yet, all these waves travel through space at the speed of light–300,000 kilometers per second (186,000 miles per second).

The spectrum of visible light consists of waves that are 0.00004 to 0.00007 centimeters long. Violet light has the shortest wavelength (0.00004 cm), while red has the longest.

Wavelengths of one millimeter to thirty centimeters are called microwaves. This portion of the electromagnetic spectrum became extremely important in the 1940s when radar was developed for use in warfare.

In 1946, the first microwave oven was built. It consisted of a radar tube that was used to cook popcorn.

MICROWAVE OVEN

If you have ever stayed in the sun too long, the sunburn you acquired is good evidence that electromagnetic waves can generate heat. The number of homes heated by solar energy is increasing at a rapid rate. There are even solar ovens that can be used to cook food, but they require bright sunshine and considerable time. However, microwave ovens can cook food very quickly any time of day.

Microwaves are generated in much the same way as radio waves. When electrons are accelerated back and forth along an antenna at a frequency of about 3,000,000 times each second, radio waves are produced. These waves travel away from the transmitter at the speed of light.

Microwaves are only about a millionth (1/1,000,000) as long as radio waves. This means that the electrons used to generate these shorter waves must move back and forth at a frequency 1,000,000 times greater than the frequency used to produce radio waves. To accelerate electrons at this rate requires a special device called a magnetron.

There is evidence that microwaves can damage human tissue; consequently, the magnetron is connected to a switch in the door of the

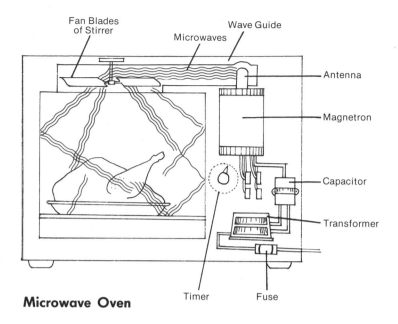

Fan Blades
of Stirrer

Wave Guide

Microwaves

Antenna

Magnetron

Capacitor

Transformer

Microwave Oven

Timer

Fuse

microwave oven. Electricity can enter the oven only after the door has been closed and latched.

When the timer is turned and set, an electric current passes through a safety fuse to a transformer. The transformer changes the 120 volts supplied by the power line to the 4,000 volts required to accelerate electrons in the magnetron. A capacitor (a cylinder made by rolling up two metal plates with an insulator between them) allows charge to be stored during the operation of the magnetron.

The microwaves leave the antenna at the top of the magnetron and travel along a wave guide. The guide channels the waves in much the same way that a megaphone enables you to direct sound waves. At the end of the wave guide, the microwaves strike the rotating metallic blades of the stirrer where they are reflected downward into the oven. There they continue to be bounced around by the metallic walls of the oven so that the food being cooked receives microwaves from all directions.

Because metal surfaces reflect microwaves, any shelves in the oven are made of glass to allow the waves to pass through.

The molecules in the uncooked food respond to the microwaves like tiny iron filings near a rotating magnet. The electric and magnetic fields that make up the microwaves change direction about 5,000,000,000 times each second. The food molecules are induced to rotate back and forth at the same rate.

Since heat is the rapid motion of molecules, the microwaves are able to cook the food by causing the molecules to rotate rapidly. In fact, food cooks much faster in a microwave oven because energy is transferred directly from the microwaves to the food molecules. In gas or electric ovens, heat is first transmitted to air molecules. The rapidly moving molecules of air collide with the food molecules, causing them to speed up. The food molecules on the surface then bump molecules that lie deeper in the food and slowly heat is conducted inward. With microwaves, energy is absorbed by molecules inside the food as well as those near the surface; therefore, food in a microwave oven is cooked throughout rather than from outside to inside.

Because microwave ovens can cook food so rapidly, the number of these ovens sold has grown rapidly over the past several years. A number of articles in books and magazines suggest that these ovens are dangerous if microwaves leak from them. Since microwaves are capable of cooking meat, it is not surprising that they damage human tissue. There is some evidence that even small amounts of microwave energy can be dangerous, particularly to the eyes. People who worked at the United States Embassy in Moscow seem to have suffered ill effects because of microwaves beamed at the Embassy building by Russian intelligence agents.

AROUND THE HOUSE

By applying an ice pack to a bad sprain, you can often prevent the joint from swelling and speed up the recovery rate. It's no wonder that coaches and trainers buy cold packs by the dozens. They are invaluable on the athletic field, and you might find them useful on a picnic or overnight hike as well.

COLD PACK, HOT PACK

For a moderate price you can buy instant "ice packs" or instant "hot-water bottles." Just sock the appropriate bag with your fist, give the bag a shake, and presto—instant ice or instant heat!

Inside the tough thick-walled outer bag is a second flimsy bag filled with some colored water. Around this inner bag is an abundant supply of some white crystals. When you hit the bag with your fist, the inner bag breaks open and the water mixed with the crystals.

You can find out what happens when the water and crystals mix by stirring some ammonium nitrate powder in water in a glass or pan. The solution that forms is cold enough to freeze drops of water on the bottom of the glass. The white crystals in the cold-pack bag are ammonium nitrate. When this chemical dissolves in water, heat is absorbed. The heat comes from the water and so the temperature of the solution becomes very cold as the crystals dissolve.

Now try dissolving some calcium chloride in water. This time the solution gets very warm. When calcium chloride and many other salts dissolve in water, heat is released. The temperature of the solution increases rapidly. This is the secret of the instant hot-water bottle.

If you try these experiments, be sure to discard the chemicals and wash the glassware thoroughly with soap and water. Both chemicals are slightly poisonous.

Air, oxygen, and nitrogen are usually gases because they boil at very low temperatures. To keep these substances that are normally gases in the liquid state they must be very cold, about −200°C (−390°F). To keep liquid air and other gases at such low temperatures, Sir James Dewar, a nineteenth-century Scottish chemist, invented the vacuum flask. Such flasks are now called Dewar flasks in his honor. They are probably known to you as Thermos bottles. While it's not likely that you use such a flask to store liquid air, you may very well use one to keep your cocoa hot or your milk cold.

There are probably more Thermos bottles in China than anywhere else in the world. The Chinese use them to keep water hot for making tea.

THERMOS BOTTLE (DEWAR FLASK)

You know that if you hold one end of a spoon and place the other end in a flame, your fingers will soon be so hot that you will drop the spoon. Heat travels along the spoon from the flame to your hand. The transmission of heat in this way is called conduction. The hot flame makes the molecules in the spoon move very fast. These rapidly moving molecules bump into their neighbors, causing them to move faster. In this way, the increased molecular motion is transmitted along the entire spoon.

Some materials such as silver, copper, iron, aluminum, and most other metals are good conductors of heat. Wood, paper, cork, wool, and Styrofoam are examples of substances that do *not* conduct heat well. Such materials are called *insulators*.

Liquids and gases are poor conductors. Porous things such as Styrofoam and cork contain many small air spaces. Since air is a poor conductor, these solid substances are good insulators too.

While gases and liquids are not good conductors of heat, we know from experience that air-filled homes can be heated when it is cold. When air in contact with a hot surface, such as a radiator, is warmed, it expands. As it expands, it becomes lighter than an equal volume of nearby cooler air. Just as a cork, a piece of wood, or a beach ball will rise if released under water, so the warm, lighter air rises as the cooler air moves under it. In

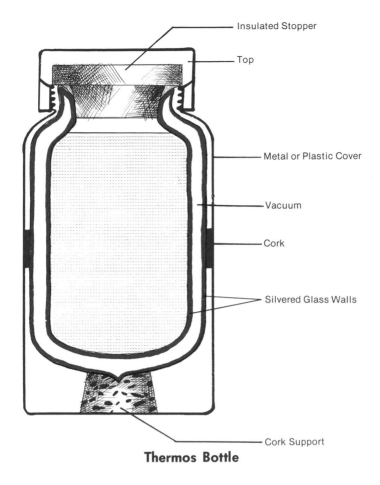

Insulated Stopper

Top

Metal or Plastic Cover

Vacuum

Cork

Silvered Glass Walls

Cork Support

Thermos Bottle

this way a current of moving air is established. The transmission of heat by moving currents of gas or liquid is called *convection*.

Radiation is the third way that heat is transmitted. The entire earth is warmed by the radiant energy from the sun. This radiant energy is similar to light and travels at the same speed. When it is absorbed by water, earth, and air, it causes the molecules of these substances to move faster. This means they are warmer. Since the space between the earth and the sun is a vacuum, there is no way that heat can be transferred from the sun to us by conduction or convection.

Most of the heat we feel from a blazing fireplace comes to us by radiation. The convection currents carry the warm air *up* the chimney, not out into the room.

51

A Thermos bottle or Dewar flask is used to store hot or cold liquids. The inside of the bottle consists of a glass vessel with two walls. The air that was in the space between the walls was removed by a vacuum pump just before the space was sealed.

If liquid is poured into such a bottle, the fluid is surrounded by a vacuum, thus heat cannot be transferred by conduction or convection. To reduce heat transmission by radiation, the glass walls are silvered. This turns the walls into mirrors that reflect any radiant energy that might enter or leave the bottle.

The neck of the bottle is where the double glass walls are connected to the cover. It is here and through the stopper that heat slowly escapes or enters the flask. To reduce the rate at which heat is conducted from or to the flask, this connection is made very small and the stopper is made of an insulating material such as cork or rubber.

If the bottle is kept in an upright position, why will the small volume of air between the liquid and the stopper reduce the rate of heat transfer through the stopper?

"Mr. Watson, come here—I want you."
Those words, spoken by Alexander Graham Bell on
March 10, 1876, were the first ever transmitted by tele-
phone. His invention led to today's world-wide network of
more than 300,000,000 telephones.

TELEPHONE

Modern telephone systems involve complex selecting and switching circuits, microwaves, and communication satellites, but the basic technology used to convert sound waves to electricity and back to sound has not changed in principle since Edison introduced the carbon microphone shortly after Bell's invention.

Speech or any sound is made by something that vibrates—vocal cords, a guitar string, a metal bell, rustling leaves, a drum, etc. The vibrating object pushes air molecules together as it moves one way and increases the distance between these molecules as it moves in the other direction. These compressed and expanded segments of air moving away from the vibrator are called sound waves (*see diagram A*).

When sound waves strike a flexible object, it too is set into motion. The sound waves from your vocal cords strike a diaphragm in the mouthpiece of a telephone. The diaphragm moves in and out with the same frequency as the sound waves that hit it. Behind the diaphragm are tiny carbon granules (*see diagram B*). The pressure within the carbon powder increases and decreases as the diaphragm moves back and forth.

When the carbon is compressed, its electrical resistance is less. This means that more electricity can flow through the carbon just as more joggers could run down a country road than a city street filled with cars and pedestrians. As the pressure on the carbon decreases, its resistance increases and less electric current flows through it. The electric current through the microphone, therefore, varies in the same way as the air pressure in the sound waves. This changing electric current is transmitted by wires to an electromagnet in the receiver earpiece.

An electromagnet is a coil of wire wound around an iron core. Whenever electricity flows through the wire a magnetic field is produced in the iron core. Even without the iron, a coil of wire carrying an electric current behaves like a bar magnet. One end of the coil acts like a north pole; the

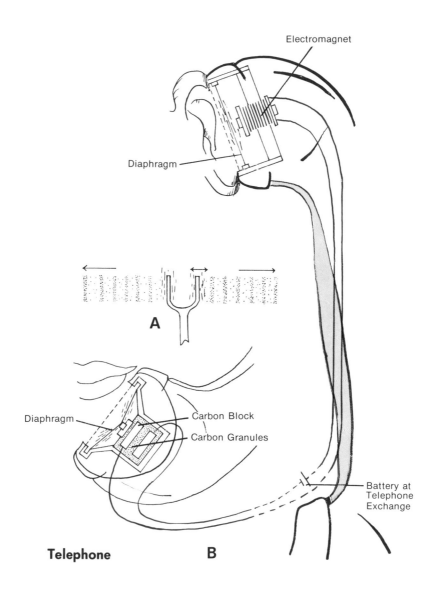

Electromagnet

Diaphragm

A

Diaphragm

Carbon Block

Carbon Granules

Battery at
Telephone
Exchange

Telephone

B

other like a south pole. The strength of the electromagnet grows with the
current in the coil. The iron core serves to concentrate and strengthen the
magnetic field.

As current in the electromagnet's coil increases, it attracts the thin metal
diaphragm in the earpiece. When the current decreases, the diaphragm
moves back. The motion of the metal diaphragm duplicates the current
surges through the electromagnet which, in turn, duplicate the pressure
waves from the sound entering the mouthpiece. Since the vibration of the

54

diaphragm in the receiver is the same as that in the microphone, the sound waves produced by the receiver diaphragm are the same as those striking the microphone, though less intense.

Sound waves spread out as they travel in all directions. They are reflected and absorbed by trees, houses, walls, mountains, and other objects. So you can't talk to someone several miles away even if you shout. Electric currents, however, will travel along a wire from one place to another. The current may have to be amplified every so often if the distance is great because electrical resistance increases as the wire lengthens, but the current does not spread out. It follows the wire and carries the message from one vibrator to another.

You reach to push open the super market door, but before you can touch it, the door springs open as if by magic.

The shadows lengthen and dusk begins to fall. Suddenly your neighbors' house lights go on; yet you know they are all away on a vacation. Later that night they return. As their car approaches the garage, the overhead door suddenly begins to rise.

A burglar forces a window open and climbs into an office. As he moves toward the safe, an alarm sounds in a nearby police station; yet he has touched nothing.

All these events are triggered by the same device, an electric eye.

ELECTRIC EYE

The setup shown in the diagram is a burglar alarm system. If anyone crosses the ultraviolet light beam that runs from the light source to the photoelectric eye, an alarm will go off.

Ultraviolet light is used in this system because it cannot be seen. (Since our eyes cannot detect light of such short wavelength, it is sometimes called "black" light.) The beam is sent around the room by reflection from mirrors. At the other end of the system, the beam falls on a photoelectric eye.

The electric eye is the key part of the system. Older electric eyes contained a photoelectric vacuum tube; modern ones have cadmium sulfide or selenium semiconductors that respond to light. When light shines on these devices, the energy in the light is transformed into the motion of electrons. The moving electrons constitute an electric current that can be magnified by an amplifier.

The amplified current flows through a relay. As long as the light beam strikes the electric eye a current flows through the electromagnet in the relay, creating a magnetic field that attracts the soft iron armature. If the beam of light is broken, as it is when a burglar steps into its path, the current from the electric eye ceases to flow. Without current, the electromagnet has no attraction for the armature, so it is pulled away by a spring and strikes a contact that starts the alarm.

56

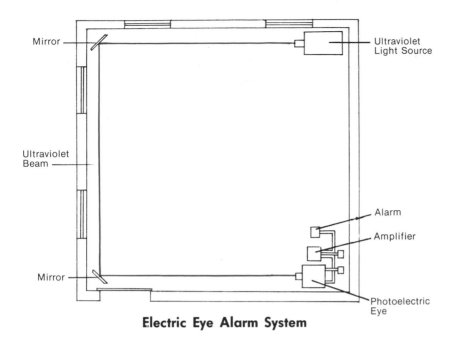

Electric Eye Alarm System

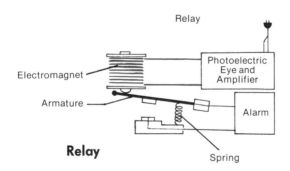

Relay

Ultraviolet light is obviously useful for burglar-alarm systems but is not used in all electric eyes. Those used to turn on house lights at dusk will respond to sunlight. Some are even sensitive to infrared light which has a wavelength that is too long for our eyes to see.

Whether used as a burglar alarm, to announce visitors, ring a buzzer, open a door, or turn a faucet off or on, the operation of electric eyes is basically the same.

In 1752, Benjamin Franklin built the world's first lightning rod and attached it to his home in Philadelphia. In 1755, in a letter to another scientist, he wrote: "I have mentioned . . . that pointed rods erected on buildings, and communicating with the moist earth, would either prevent a stroke (lightning), or, if not prevented, would conduct it, so that the building should suffer no damage."

LIGHTNING RODS

Lightning rods are widely used today and have greatly reduced the damage caused by lightning. Nevertheless, lightning remains a threat to life and property. It kills over 150 people in the United States each year, destroys over $20,000,000 worth of property, and sets about 10,000 forest fires that burn $30,000,000 worth of timber.

There is no foolproof way to prevent lightning from striking your house, but you can provide a path that will conduct the lightning safely to ground. A lightning rod and conductor will protect a house in an electric storm, but how does it work? To answer this question, we need to know a little bit about lightning and what causes it.

You've probably seen and felt mini-lightning flashes many times. They are common in the winter when the air in your house is very dry. Perhaps you took off a pullover sweater in a dark room and saw sparks. Or you may have reached for a metal door handle and saw, felt, and heard a spark jump between the handle and your hand.

Before you reached for the door, you may have walked across a rug. The friction between you and the rug caused you to acquire, let's say, some positive electric charge. Now, there are two kinds of charge, positive and negative. Positive charges will attract negative charges and repel other positive charges. Similarly, negative charges also repel one another but attract positive charges.

When you reach for the door, the negative charges in the metal are pulled toward the positive charges in your hand. The attractive force gets very much larger as the charges move closer together. Finally, the force becomes so great that the negative charges (electrons) flow across the short air space to unite with and neutralize the positive charges in your hand.

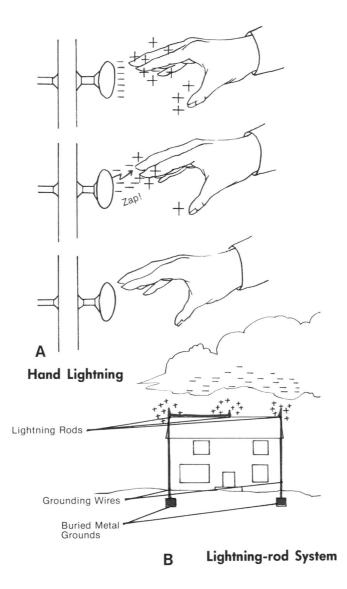

A
Hand Lightning

Lightning Rods

Grounding Wires

Buried Metal
Grounds

B   **Lightning-rod System**

The air along the path is heated, expands, and then contracts as it cools. The snap you hear is created by sound waves produced when the air masses around the spark collide as the air cools and contracts. With lightning, the spark becomes a very large flash or bolt and the snap becomes a thunderclap.

During the formation of thunderclouds, positive and negative charges are separated. The most common form of lightning flash occurs when charge flows across the space between two oppositely charged clouds.

Charges of opposite sign (positive and negative) attract, so a negatively charged cloud will attract positive charges from the ground. These charges will try to get as close to the negatively charged cloud as possible. The attracted charges will concentrate on sharp points and corners. For these reasons, and because electricity flows best along metals, lightning rods are made of metal with their upper ends pointed and placed higher than anything else on the building. The lightning rods' pointed tips offer a greater attraction for the charges in the cloud than the material in the building.

Most lightning-rod systems have several points that connect with two or more grounding wires. There are also metal connections between the rods and water and heating pipes within the building to be sure the lightning flash does not travel between the lightning conductors and these grounded metallic pipes.

Steel-framed buildings generally do not need lightning rods because the steel will conduct any lightning discharge to earth.

An automobile is a fairly safe place to be during a thunder storm but *not* because the car has rubber tires. In fact, a large number of farmers are killed every year when struck by lightning while riding on rubber-tired tractors. The reason a car is so safe is that you are surrounded by metal and there are no electrical effects inside a metal box or cage.

Since charge from ground that is opposite in sign to the charge on a cloud will try to get as close as possible to the cloud because opposite charges attract, lightning usually strikes an object that is closer to the cloud than anything else. Seeking refuge under a tree, riding atop a tractor, or even standing in an open field is *not* a safe measure to take during a thunderstorm.

If you are outside as a thunderstorm approaches, seek shelter in a house or car, or try to get to low ground. If lightning is nearby, crouch near the ground and keep your feet together. If your feet are apart, electricity may find your body an easier path than the ground between your feet.

Luigi Galvani (1737–98), an Italian professor of anatomy, noticed that the muscles in a frog's leg would twitch not only when touched by an electric spark but whenever they were in contact with two different metals. Galvani believed that the electricity came from the muscles, but Alessandro Volta (1745–1827) proved that it came from the two metals. He was able to produce electricity by placing strips of zinc and copper in bowls of salt solution. To make a more portable source of electricity, he used small disks of copper and zinc. He placed these disks alternately in a pile with small round pieces of cardboard soaked in salt solution between them. This "voltaic pile" was used by William Nicholson (1735–1815), an English chemist, to electrolyze water into hydrogen and oxygen.

ELECTRIC CELLS: A BATTERY

A piece of shiny zinc metal is placed in a beautiful blue solution of copper sulfate. The zinc becomes coated with an orange-red powder. Slowly, the zinc disappears and the solution's blue color fades. We are left with a clear liquid and a pile of orange-red powder. This is a chemical reaction. Substances have disappeared and new substances have been formed. Zinc has reacted with copper sulfate. The orange-red powder produced is copper metal. If the clear solution is allowed to evaporate, a white powder that is zinc sulfate will appear.

This chemical reaction releases energy, but it appears as heat which is of little use in such a slow reaction. However, if we arrange the chemicals as shown in the diagram, the same reaction will take place, but much of the energy will appear as electricity which can be used to light bulbs, turn motors, operate calculators, etc.

In the electric cell shown, zinc metal is placed in a solution of zinc

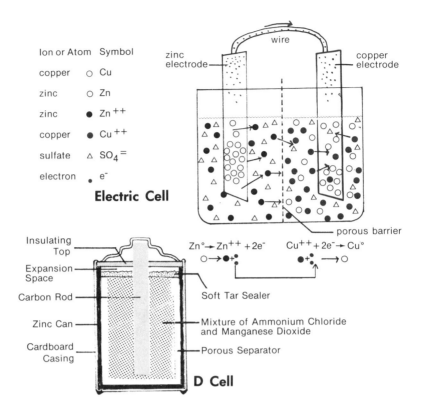

Ion or Atom	Symbol
copper	○ Cu
zinc	○ Zn
zinc	● Zn^{++}
copper	● Cu^{++}
sulfate	△ $SO_4^{=}$
electron	• e^-

Electric Cell

zinc electrode

wire

copper electrode

porous barrier

$Zn° \rightarrow Zn^{++} + 2e^-$ $Cu^{++} + 2e^- \rightarrow Cu°$

Insulating Top

Expansion Space

Carbon Rod

Zinc Can

Cardboard Casing

Soft Tar Sealer

Mixture of Ammonium Chloride and Manganese Dioxide

Porous Separator

D Cell

sulfate and a copper strip is placed in copper sulfate solution. The two metals are connected by a wire and the two solutions separated by a porous divider. An ammeter will show that electricity flows in the circuit; in fact, electrons flow from zinc to copper. Zinc gives up electrons more readily than copper. It is the negative pole of this electric cell.

Zinc atoms in the metal give up two electrons which flow along the wire to the copper metal. Since the electrons are negatively charged, the zinc atoms each acquire a charge of $+2$. These charged atoms are called zinc ions. They are soluble and go into the zinc sulfate solution where ions of zinc as well as negative sulfate ions ($SO_4^{=}$) already exist.

The positively charged copper ions (Cu^{++}) in the copper sulfate solution are attracted to the electrons flowing onto the copper metal. They each combine with two negative particles (electrons) to form neutral copper atoms which stick to (plate on) the copper electrode (the positive pole of the cell).

The porous barrier retards the flow of copper sulfate toward the zinc electrode and enables zinc ions to move into the copper sulfate solution. These ions replace the positive copper ions that are removed from the solution. If the zinc were in direct contact with the copper sulfate, the electrons would flow directly from the zinc to the copper ions without passing along the wire.

An electric cell, then, is a device that converts the energy of a chemical reaction into electricity. It does this by separating the reacting chemicals in such a way that electrons must move along a wire to be transferred from an atom to a positive ion.

When electric cells are hooked in series (+ to − to + to −, etc.), they form a battery. But people often speak of a single electric cell as a battery. D cells, for instance, are often called flashlight "batteries."

Flashlight batteries are perhaps the most common and best-known electric cell. As the diagram shows, the zinc case is the negative electrode. Electrons flow to a carbon rod, but it is the positive ammonium ions (NH_4^+) in the moist mixture of ammonium chloride and manganese dioxide that the electrons neutralize. The hydrogen released when ammonium ions are neutralized tends to collect around the carbon rod polarizing the cell (preventing the flow of charge). The black manganese dioxide serves to reduce polarization because it reacts with the hydrogen gas to form water and another oxide of manganese.

Flashlight cells are primary cells. They cannot be recharged, but the cells in lead storage batteries are examples of secondary cells. Here the chemical reactions can be forced to run in the opposite direction and the discharged battery restored to its original condition. These heavy-duty batteries are used in automobiles and are essential to the operation of electric cars.

*During the revolutionary war and for many years thereaf-
ter, the normal method of starting a fire was to rub flint
against steel to ignite small pieces of combustible material called tinder. Tinderboxes were found by nearly
every fireplace. In 1826, John Walker invented the "lucifer." Lucifers were sticks coated at one end with a
paste made from antimony sulfide, potassium chloride,
gum, and water. When the paste was dry, the lucifer
could be ignited by pulling it through a piece of folded
sandpaper.*

MATCHES

"Strike anywhere" or "kitchen" matches are made from blocks of
thoroughly seasoned white pine. The blocks are cut into sticks and fed into
a rotating belt that carries the sticks through a series of automatic proc-
esses. First, the sticks are submerged in a solution of ammonium phos-
phate that will prevent the match from glowing after it has been blown out.
(You may have found some matches that probably were not very well
impregnated with this solution.)

After drying, the matches are dipped in liquid paraffin. (You may have
encountered matches that behave as though they were dipped in water.)
The ends of the matches are then dipped in a liquid mixture of potassium
chlorate, sulfur, clay, glue, and coloring to form the match heads. When
the match heads are partially dry, the tips of the matches are dipped into a
similar mixture that contains a large amount of phosphorus trisulfide. This
forms the "eye" of the match—the part you rub to ignite it.

The matches are thoroughly dried and placed side by side in boxes. The
large heads prevent the eyes or tips of the matches from rubbing against
one another and igniting.

When the tip of the match is rubbed along a rough surface, the friction
produces enough heat to ignite the phosphorus trisulfide. This burning, in
turn, heats the potassium chlorate, which releases oxygen as it decomposes. The oxygen together with the heat ignites the sulfur. The flame
produced in the match head spreads to the flammable paraffin-soaked stick.

If you look closely at safety matches, you will find that they do not
have a tip or eye. Instead, the head is uniformly coated with a combustible

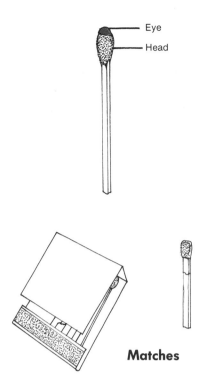

Matches

mixture of substances such as antimony trisulfide and potassium dichromate held together with glue. The striking surface on the matchbook contains red phosphorus and powdered glass mixed with glue.

Friction between the match head and the striking surface produces enough heat to decompose the potassium dichromate, releasing oxygen. The oxygen combines with the phosphorus during the short time they are in contact, and the heat from this combustion ignites the antimony trisulfide.

Safety matches will not ignite very easily because the phosphorus which is easily ignited is on the striking surface, not the match. Only a few particles of phosphorus rub off the surface and ignite as oxygen is released from potassium dichromate.

In 1893, Whitcomb Judson filed a patent for a "slide fastener," but zippers did not become popular before 1930. It wasn't until 1926 that the "zipper" got its name. Gilbert Frankau is reported to have said, at an exhibit promoting these slide fasteners, "Zip! It's open! Zip! It's closed!" The name stuck, but not, we hope, the zipper.

ZIPPERS

A zipper has three parts: many small identical metal or plastic "teeth" or hooks, a pair of fabric strips that can be stitched to clothing, and a Y-shaped slider that opens and closes the fastener.

The teeth are clamped along the two strips of textile material at equally spaced intervals. The teeth on the two strips are staggered so that a tooth on one side is opposite the space between teeth on the other side. Each tooth has a protrusion on its top side and a hollow on its lower side. The protrusion on one tooth fits into the hollow on a tooth that lies above it on the adjoining strip of fabric (*see diagram*). Once the teeth are joined, they cannot slip apart because the protrusion is too big to fit through the space between the teeth.

If you don't think it's hard to fit the teeth together, try doing it by hand. You'll soon appreciate the value of the slider that quickly locks and unlocks the intermeshing teeth of the zipper. The slider has two channels at its top that merge at the bottom. The angle between the two channels is made so that opposing teeth can be brought together or separated.

Look carefully at the diagram. You will see that as a tooth moves into the upper part of the Y channel, the space between it and the tooth below it increases. A tooth on the opposite strip of fabric can fit between these two teeth. The teeth will lock when they are brought together in the single channel.

When the zipper is completely closed, the last few teeth lie within the two channels of the Y-shaped slide so that the teeth can be unlocked as the slide is pulled downward. If all the teeth were linked, there would be no way the slide could get between the teeth and establish the proper angle between the fabric strips for unzipping.

Most zipper slides can be locked by turning the handle of the slide back against the teeth.

66

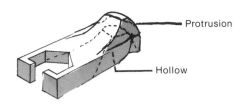

Protrusion

Hollow

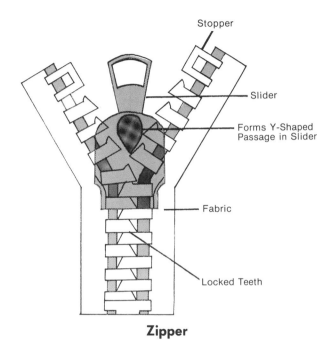

Stopper

Slider

Forms Y-Shaped
Passage in Slider

Fabric

Locked Teeth

Zipper

The two strips of teeth on the zippers of jackets are usually made so that the strips can be separated and the jacket easily removed. One side of these zippers has a short metal bar at its lower end. This little metal bar fits into the slide located on the opposite zipper strip (usually the right side). It slides past the Y-shaped channel into the left slot of a small piece of metal that is permanently fixed to the right side of the zipper. A similar metal bar on the right zipper strip is clamped to a parallel slot in the metal base.

Zippers have become so common that we often forget what ingenious timesaving devices they are.

MEDICINE AND HEALTH

Breathing was the first of the vital functions essential to life to be carried out by a machine. A simple respirator operated with a hand pump was used for resuscitation as early as 1876. In 1929, Philip Drinker invented an airtight box that could be used to replace the muscles normally used in breathing.

IRON AND ARTIFICIAL LUNGS

To illustrate the breathing process, you can build the model shown in the diagram. The balloons represent your lungs, the glass jar your chest, the rubber sheet the diaphragm that separates your chest from your abdomen, and the glass tube your trachea (the cartilage-covered tube that you can feel in the front of your throat). When you pull the "diaphragm" down, the pressure around the outside of the balloons decreases because the air molecules inside the jar have more space in which to move around. Therefore, the molecules bump into the balloon less often and so there is less pressure. When this happens, the pressure of the air outside the jar becomes greater than the pressure around the balloons. This causes air to rush into the balloons and inflate them. When the diaphragm is released, the pressure inside the jar increases because the gas around the balloons is squeezed into a smaller space. The balloons deflate and air is forced out the "trachea."

A similar process takes place when you breathe. Your diaphragm contracts and muscles pull your ribs upward and outward. This makes your lungs bigger and reduces the pressure of the air inside them. Because the air pressure is now greater than the pressure of the air in your lungs, air is inhaled.

To exhale, we simply relax our rib muscles and diaphragm. The decreased volume of the chest cavity forces air out of the lungs. Unlike the balloons in the glass jar, your lungs do not collapse. They are attached to the inside of your chest wall and so get no smaller than your chest cavity will allow.

71

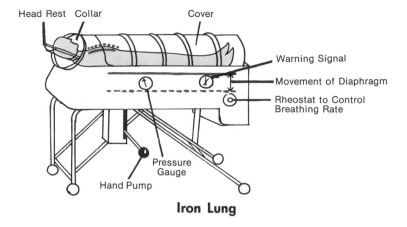

Head Rest Collar   Cover

Warning Signal

Movement of Diaphragm

Rheostat to Control
Breathing Rate

Pressure
Gauge

Hand Pump

Iron Lung

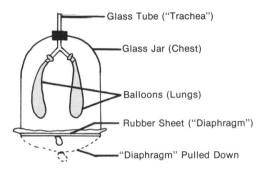

Glass Tube ("Trachea")

Glass Jar (Chest)

Balloons (Lungs)

Rubber Sheet ("Diaphragm")

"Diaphragm" Pulled Down

Model of Lungs

If paralysis or something else prevents someone from breathing normally, he or she may be placed in an iron lung. This machine will cause the person to breathe automatically.

The person lies on a bed in the iron lung. His or her head sticks out of one end of the machine. A rubber collar at the base of the person's neck forms an airtight seal between the inside and outside of the machine.

Beneath the bed, a diaphragm is moved up and down about fifteen times a minute by an electric motor. As the diaphragm moves upward, the space occupied by the air in the machine is reduced. This increases the pressure of the air inside the machine which squeezes the patient's body, forcing air from his or her lungs. When the diaphragm moves downward, the pressure inside the machine decreases and the patient's chest returns to its normal size and air rushes back into the expanding lungs.

72

Should a power failure stop the electric motor, an alarm sounds and the iron lung must be operated by hand.

If a doctor wants to examine the patient, the top of the iron lung can be removed. The patient's head is placed in a plastic dome. Tubes from the dome are connected to a pump that pushes air in and out of the lungs. This is similar to mouth-to-mouth resuscitation, which is used in emergencies when someone cannot breathe.

You can get a feeling for the way an iron lung works by having someone squeeze your chest (not too hard) with his or her arms and then suddenly releasing the pressure. Air will enter your lungs as your chest springs back to its normal size. What happens to the air in your lungs while you are being squeezed?

While the iron lung is useful in saving the lives of people who have lost the ability to breathe because of damage to their nervous system, it is of no value to patients whose lungs cannot function. If the lungs are filled with smoke (smoke inhalation) or fluid (drowning or pneumonia), an iron lung is useless, because gases cannot pass easily between the blood and the air in the lungs.

Some very promising experimental work has been done with an artificial lung, a device that does the lung's work outside the body. In this machine, blood is taken out of the jugular vein in the neck and routed through a series of tubes that grow progressively smaller. When the blood reaches some tubes made of very thin silicone rubber, the oxygen that surrounds these thin membranes can pass through them and enter the blood. At the same time the waste product carbon dioxide that has collected in the blood will move across the membranes in the opposite direction. After passing through these membranes, the blood flows into progressively larger tubes until it is sent back into the body through an artery in the patient's leg.

Because blood frequently clots when it passes through artificial tubes, a chemical called heparin is added to the blood to reduce the possibility of this happening. Unfortunately, heparin's ability to prevent clotting also raises the danger of internal bleeding. Consequently, the amount of heparin added to the blood must be carefully controlled.

Each beat of your heart sends blood rushing through the valves that separate the auricles from the ventricles, the left ventricle from the aortic artery, and the right ventricle from the pulmonary artery. The "lub-dub" sound of the heartbeat is the result of these valves being slammed shut by the pressure of the blood.

The human heart contracts about 70 times each minute, 4,200 times every hour, 100,000 times each day, 40,000,-000 times a year, and 30,000,000,000 times in a normal life span. Is it any wonder that valves opening and closing so often occasionally become defective?

ARTIFICIAL HEART VALVES

The human heart is a four-chambered pump powered by a mass of muscle tissue about the size of your fist. A series of valves allows blood to pass in only one direction: from the right auricle (RA), to the right ventricle (RV), to the pulmonary artery (PA), to the lungs (L), where the blood is replenished with oxygen as it discards excess carbon dioxide, then back to the left aurical (LA), to the left ventricle (LV), and finally through the aortic valve into the aortic artery (A). From here blood travels through branch arteries and arterioles to capillaries (C) where molecules of gases, liquids, and solids dissolved in blood and tissue fluid are exchanged. The capillaries join to form small veins that unite to form large veins (V) leading back to the heart's right auricle.

The tricuspid and bicuspid valves open as the auricles contract, forcing blood into the ventricles. When the ventricles contract, the flaps of these valves are pushed together by the rising blood pressure. With the valves closed, blood cannot re-enter the auricles. Instead, it pushes open the semilunar valves that guard the openings into the pulmonary and aortic arteries, forcing these vessels to expand.

As the heart muscle enters its resting stage following each contraction, the stretched arterial walls contract. This creates a back pressure that slams the one-way semilunar valves shut and squeezes the blood along the arteries away from the heart.

When ill-formed or damaged valves allow blood to leak back into the auricles or ventricles, the efficiency of the circulatory system diminishes to

74

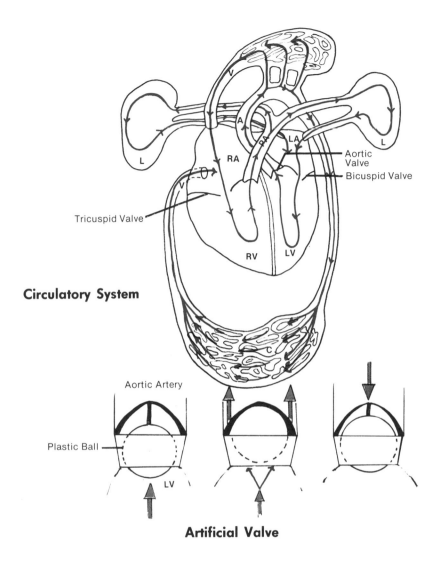

Circulatory System

Aortic Valve

Bicuspid Valve

Tricuspid Valve

RA

RV

LV

LA

V

A

L

L

L

Aortic Artery

Plastic Ball

LV

Artificial Valve

a point that may endanger a person's health or his or her ability to lead an active life. Thirty years ago such a person would have had to lead a very sedentary life-style. Today, such valves may be surgically repaired or artificial valves such as the ball-and-socket valve shown in the diagram may be used to replace a defective one.

In the valve shown in the diagram blood pressure created by a contracting heart will push the plastic ball out of the ring that is sewed into the aortic artery where it joins the left ventricle. Blood flows by the ball into the artery. When the heart muscle relaxes and the arterial walls contract, the back flow of blood toward the heart forces the ball back into the ring. The blood then must flow away from the heart along the artery as it should. Before the valve was installed, some blood moved back into the heart through the patient's faulty semilunar flaps.

Similar valves may be used to reduce leakage from the ventricles into the auricles or from the pulmonary artery into the right ventricle. These valves may enable a patient to enjoy a much more active life, but his or her diet may have to be carefully controlled. A plastic valve is a foreign body, and certain chemicals in the blood may accumulate on the valve and prevent the ball from seating properly in the ring.

Dr. W. H. Walshe first suggested using electricity to regulate and stimulate the heartbeat in 1862. Seventy years later, Dr. A. S. Hyman developed what he called an "artificial cardiac pacemaker." It weighed nearly 16 pounds (7.2 kilograms). Modern electronics makes it possible to build pacemakers weighing just a few grams that can be implanted in a patient's chest.

PACEMAKER

Normally your heartbeat is controlled by electrical impulses that come from the heart itself. Stimuli from the central nervous system speed up the heart's pacemaker when you are active and slow it down when you are resting. But even if your heart were cut off from all nerves, it would, unlike other muscles in your body, continue to contract. However, it would not beat seventy times per minute as it normally does. Instead, the auricles would contract fifty to sixty times each minute, while the ventricles, beating independently, would contract eighteen to thirty times. Such a slow beat cannot keep a person alive. Doctors today often use an artificial pacemaker to regulate the heartbeat of a person whose heart is not beating normally.

The first successful pacemakers, used in the 1950s, were worn outside the body. Wires ran from the pacemaker batteries and circuit through the skin into the heart muscle. Unfortunately, sooner or later an infection would develop along the flesh around the wires. It became clear that pacemakers would have to be implanted in the body for long-term use.

In most modern pacemakers, the batteries, transistors, and integrated circuits, which are about the size of a man's thumb, are placed under the skin in the patient's chest. A thin wire from the pacemaker circuit is threaded down a neck vein, into the right auricle, through the tricuspid valve, to a relatively motionless part of the right ventricle. The end of this wire serves as an electrode through which the pacemaker sends electrical impulses to the heart.

The average current for each electrical impulse is only one to two milliamperes, so the pacemaker batteries need produce less than fifty millionths of a kilowatt-hour of energy per year. Because very little power is needed to operate a pacemaker, the mercury batteries will last for two to three years.

Many pacemakers today are powered by nuclear batteries. A 400-milligram pellet of plutonium 238 generates the heat needed to run a thermocouple. A thermocouple consists of two *different* metals soldered together at a junction (*see diagram*). If the junction is heated while the ends of the wires remain cool, electric charges of opposite sign collect at the free ends of the two wires just as they do at the poles of a battery.

The radiation produced by these batteries is no greater than that found in watches with luminous dials, but the heating effect of the plutonium can power the pacemaker for ten years. People with plutonium-powered pacemakers will not have to have new batteries buried under the skin in their chests every two to three years.

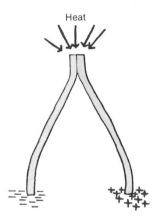

Thermocouple

If a heart is severely damaged, surgeons may remove the organ and replace it with the heart of someone who has recently died. This transplant operation which was popular a few years ago has become less common. After a few months the body tends to reject the foreign tissue.

Surgeons are striving to build an artificial heart that can replace one that is worn out. This is a difficult task. Such a pump must be able to repeat its cycle 40,000,000 times each year without breaking down. It must be tough, flexible, and have no effect on the blood that passes through it, nor should the heart be affected by the blood. Finally, the rate at which the heart beats must respond to the body's need.

78

A number of different materials and designs are now being tested with animals, but the requirements for such a heart are difficult to achieve. The human heart, after all, is a truly miraculous organ.

Open-heart surgery requires not only the skillful hands of superb surgeons, but the amazing technology of a machine that does the work of the patient's heart and lungs so that doctors can work on a blood-free heart for an hour or more. This machine must pump the blood at proper pressure, maintain its temperature at 37°C (98.6°F) or lower it to 8°C (46°F), remove waste carbon dioxide from, and supply fresh oxygen to, the flowing blood, prevent the blood from clotting or picking up air bubbles, and keep damage to red blood cells at a minimum.

HEART-LUNG MACHINE

Technicians have checked and sterilized the heart-lung machine as they prepare for open-heart surgery. The tubes are filled with sterile fluid and the tube endings wrapped in plastic bags.

The patient is brought in and surgery begins. Tubes from the machine are connected to tubes leading from the patient's two major veins, aortic artery, and coronary (heart) arteries. First, the clamps on the tubes from the blood vessels are opened, then, after a check reveals no air bubbles in the lines, the valves into the machine's tubes are opened and the pump started (*see diagram*). The pump is started and circulates blood together with the heart. When the machine is found to be working satisfactorily, surgeons clamp the major veins leading to the heart at points close to the organ. Next, they clamp the aortic artery to prevent any backflow into the left ventricle. Finally, they release the clamps on the tubes connecting the return lines from the machine to the coronary arteries. These arteries branch off the aortic artery just after its union with the heart and supply the heart muscle with the blood.

Technicians and nurses constantly monitor the patient's blood pressure, urine production, and other vital signs as the doctors repair the heart. Since there is no blood flow through the heart's chambers, they can see the tissue clearly and so work quickly and effectively while the machine circulates the blood.

Blood entering the machine from the major veins flows through an oxygenator where rotating stainless steel disks carry a thin film of blood

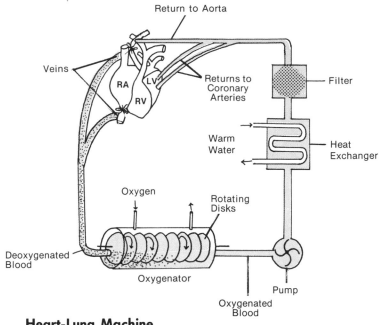

Heart-Lung Machine

into contact with oxygen. The disks spread the blood out over a large area so that oxygen can make contact with red blood cells. The hemoglobin in these cells combines with oxygen while excess carbon dioxide diffuses out of the blood. As the blood picks up oxygen, it develops the bright red color characteristic of arterial blood. The "lungs" have done their job and the blood enters the "heart" of the machine.

The machine's pump is designed to damage as few blood cells as possible. It has no slam-shut valves, sharp corners, or nozzles. Blood flows smoothly through the pump. Despite all the precautions, a considerable number of cells are destroyed. The smoothest plastic tubing and valves made are very rough compared to the natural lining of blood vessels and the surface of heart valves.

Because the blood travels through two meters (6½ feet) of tubing in a room at 20°C (68°F), it cools slightly and must be warmed before it returns to the patient's arteries. In the heat exchanger, warm water passes over the blood-filled tubing, bringing the blood temperature back to 37°C (98.6°F). Sometimes the heat exchanger is used to cool the patient's blood.

Finally, the blood is filtered to remove any clots and air bubbles before it returns to the patient's aorta and coronary arteries.

After surgeons have repaired the heart, the patient is carefully disconnected from the machine. As soon as the doctors are sure the heart is working properly, the chest cavity is closed and the patient moved to an intensive care unit.

Any blood remaining in the machine may be removed and bottled. It can be transferred back into the patient's body during recovery. The machine is then washed, sterilized, and made ready for future use.

Willem Kolff invented the first artificial kidney in Holland in 1944. Today tens of thousands of people with defective kidneys spend four to eight hours, three days each week, connected to a kidney machine that cleanses their blood. Many of these people have portable machines that they use at home or on trips. Some seek a kidney transplant to free them from their dependence on a machine. Others, fearing the tissue rejection common to organ transplants, prefer the safety of the kidney machine even though they do not enjoy the same vitality they had when their kidneys worked.

ARTIFICIAL KIDNEY

Kidneys are a pair of organs, each about the size of your fist, that lie against the back of the lower abdominal cavity. They serve as the body's filters, removing water and waste products from the blood to form urine which is stored in the bladder before being excreted. The tiny units that do the filtering are called *nephrons*. There are about a million of these in each kidney. One such unit is shown in the diagram.

Blood from an artery (A) flows into a tuft of capillaries called the glomerulus (G). Water and wastes diffuse from the blood into the expanded end of a tubule, called Bowman's capsule (B), that surrounds much of the glomerulus. The fluid entering the capsule flows along the proximal convoluted tubule (PCT), through Henle's loop (HL) and the distal convoluted tubule (DCT), to the collecting tubule (CT) which leads to the bladder. During its passage through these tubules, some water and chemicals re-enter the blood.

An artificial kidney can duplicate the simple filtering process between the glomerulus and Bowman's capsule, but it cannot bring about the selective reabsorption of chemicals that occurs in the convoluted tubules.

When a patient is connected to an artificial kidney, blood is removed through a Teflon tube that is permanently connected to an artery and vein. A small amount of a chemical called heparin is added to the blood to prevent it from clotting. The blood is pumped through a long thin plastic membrane filled with tiny pores. The pores are slightly larger than water,

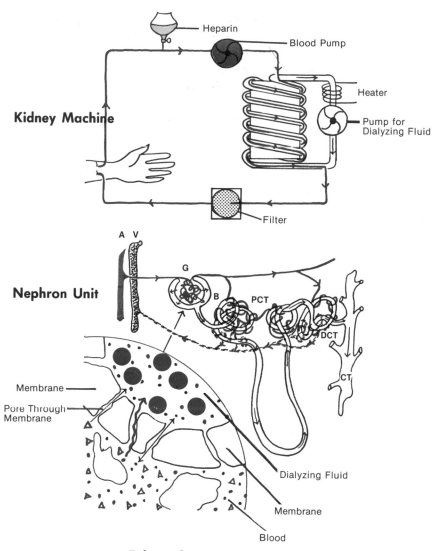

Kidney Machine

Heparin

Blood Pump

Heater

Pump for Dialyzing Fluid

Filter

Nephron Unit

A V

G

B

PCT

DCT

CT

Membrane

Pore Through Membrane

Dialyzing Fluid

Membrane

Blood

Enlarged View of Membrane

urea, and other waste molecules so these substances can pass through the membrane.

Substances will diffuse (spread) if there are more of them in one place than another. To illustrate, consider two large goldfish bowls with a connecting tunnel between them. If you place a hundred goldfish in one bowl and one in the other, you will find fish move into the empty bowl until there are about fifty in each bowl. After this there will be about as many fish moving one way as the other.

The same thing happens through the pores of the thin membrane that encloses the blood in the kidney machine. A dialyzing fluid (one that will promote diffusion) flows over the thin membrane in a direction opposite that of the blood. The fluid has few or no waste molecules such as urea in it, but it does contain sugars and salts that the body needs in exactly the same concentration as in the blood. As the two fluids flow by one another, waste molecules (shown as colored triangles in the diagram) will diffuse from the blood to the dialyzing fluids. Since sugars and salts (black dots) essential to the body have the same concentration in both liquids, there will be no net diffusion of these substances.

Large protein molecules (globular structures in the diagram) and blood cells are much too large to pass through the pores, so they remain in the blood as they should. Large sugar molecules (colored circles in the diagram) can't fit through the pores. They are added to the dialyzing fluid to cause osmosis—the movement of water through a semipermeable membrane. The water molecules are represented by small colored circles, their path through the pores by small wavy lines.

The movement of water across the membrane promotes the diffusion of waste molecules because it generates a small current through the pores. The filtration is also quickened by keeping the blood at a higher pressure than the dialyzing fluid. The higher blood pressure is a safety measure. Should a leak develop in the membrane, the unsterile dialyzing fluid will not enter and contaminate the blood.

Once blood has passed over the membrane, it is filtered to remove any air bubbles or clots before it re-enters the patient's bloodstream.

People with acute kidney failure are kept on a low-rate dialysis machine for a period of days. Those with chronic kidney failure can survive by using the machine two or three times a week for a few hours if they follow a strict diet that produces very little blood-carried waste products. People have lived for as long as ten days with no kidney action before succumbing to toxemia (poisoning).

The search for better, less expensive, more flexible kidneys continues. One recent method is to pour dialyzing fluid into the abdominal cavity through a capped plastic tube. The fluid sloshes around inside, passing over the numerous capillaries in the lining of the body wall, extracting wastes as it moves. After a few hours it is drained out of the same tube. Patients who have tried this method like it because they can remain active during dialysis.

*On November 8, 1895, Wilhelm Röntgen accidentally dis-
covered X-rays. He noticed that fluorescent crystals on
the other side of the dark room where he was working
would glow when he turned on his electric discharge
tube. He reasoned that some kind of invisible penetrating
rays were being produced by the tube. Since he didn't
know what these rays were, he called them X-rays.
Today we know that X-rays are electromagnetic waves
with very short wavelengths. So short are these waves
that over 100,000 of them would fit into one wavelength
of visible light which is less than 0.0001 centimeter long.*

X-RAY TUBE

Within months after Röntgen's discovery, X-rays were being used to photograph broken bones, locate a bullet in a person's leg, and distinguish between real and artificial gems.

You have probably had X-rays of your teeth or bones. Next time your dentist X-rays your teeth, ask him to let you look at the negatives. Your teeth appear white on the film because very little of the radiation reached the film through your teeth. The fleshy tissue appears dark because X-rays can penetrate through skin and muscle. But how does the X-ray machine that your dentist uses work?

Inside the machine is an X-ray tube. The tube has an incandescent filament in the cathode (*see diagram*) which is heated by a low-voltage source. The electrons that "boil" off the filament are attracted to the positively charged anode or target. The cathode is concave in order to focus electrons on the anode. A transformer establishes a voltage of 10,000 to 2,000,000 volts between the cathode and anode. By the time electrons reach the anode, they are moving very fast. The sudden stopping of the electrons when they hit the anode converts the energy of motion into X-rays. The radiation passes through a window to the object being photographed. A film enclosed in a light-tight holder is placed behind or below the object.

The ability of X-rays to pass through or penetrate matter depends on the voltage used to produce the X-rays and the density of the material through which the radiation must travel. X-rays of short wavelength are produced

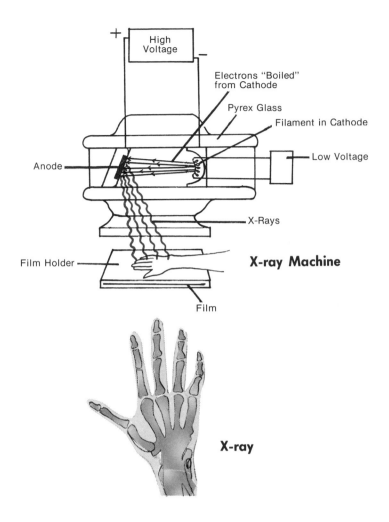

X-ray Machine

Labels on diagram:
+ / − High Voltage
Electrons "Boiled" from Cathode
Pyrex Glass
Filament in Cathode
Low Voltage
Anode
X-Rays
Film Holder
Film

X-ray

by using a high voltage. They are called *hard* X-rays. *Soft* X-rays have a longer wavelength and are produced by using a lower voltage. The harder the X-rays, the more penetrating they are.

Bones contain a large amount of calcium and are good absorbers of X-rays. Flesh contains mostly lighter elements such as carbon, oxygen, hydrogen, and nitrogen, and is a very poor absorber. This explains why the shadows cast by bones appear much whiter on the photographic film (negative) than flesh. If a print (ordinary photograph) is made from the negative, the bones will appear darker than the flesh (*see diagram*).

87

Internal organs such as the stomach and intestines are often filled with a good X-ray absorber such as barium sulfate solution before an X-ray photograph is made. This makes the organs much easier to see on the negative.

X-rays are also used in treating some tumors and cancers that are often good absorbers of X-rays and may be destroyed without serious damage to the normal surrounding tissue.

In addition to their medical uses, X-rays are used to sterilize and analyze materials, study crystals, determine the size of small particles, examine building materials for defects in castings and weldings, produce mutations in experimental animals, and in an ever-growing number of industrial and research techniques.

Röntgen's accidental discovery of X-rays gave rise to one of the most important tools in modern medicine and scientific research.

RECREATION

The nearly frictionless quality of ice is essential for both the graceful movements of accomplished figure skaters and the awesome speed of those pros who play the world's fastest game.

Tabletop hockey is not played on ice, but a simple invention has provided a playing surface that has even less friction than ice.

TABLETOP OR AIR HOCKEY

Playing tabletop hockey on a floor or table is like skating on wood—very slow, very tiring, and not much fun. But if you have played modern tabletop or air hockey, you know that the surface makes the game very fast and a lot of fun. It may tire you out but it's certainly not tedious.

Why does the plastic puck move over the playing surface so easily with no sign of slowing down?

Look carefully at the playing surface. You will see a lot of small holes about an inch apart over the entire surface. Turn on the switch and place a tuft of cotton or a small piece of paper near one of the holes. The cotton will "dance" about, indicating that a gas is coming out the holes. Turn off the switch and the dancing stops. What is the gas and why is it there? Why is there no gas unless the switch is turned on?

Beneath the table is an electric motor that drives one or two blower fans. It is similar to the exhaust fans over a kitchen range or in a vacuum cleaner. The fans pull in air and force it into a space beneath the tabletop called a plenum. The air entering the plenum strikes a baffle that spreads the moving gas throughout the space beneath the tabletop. As air enters the plenum the pressure increases. The only exits for the gas are the tiny holes through the surface of the table. Thus, the very smooth tabletop becomes covered with a series of closely spaced tiny air jets.

The plastic puck used to play the game rests on the air streams. As the air jets strike the bottom of the puck, the air spreads out beneath the puck,

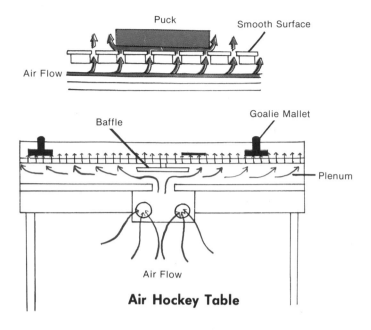

Puck
Smooth Surface
Air Flow

Baffle
Goalie Mallet
Plenum
Air Flow

Air Hockey Table

forming a very thin layer of gas that raises the puck off the table. The puck actually floats on a thin layer of air. Because it does not touch the table, there is practically no friction to slow the puck down. If you hit the puck with your goalie mallet and give it a certain speed, it will continue to move at this speed because there is nothing to stop it.

The simple method of reducing friction is not limited to games or science demonstrations. It has been used in other ways too. Huge fans in the bases of Hovercrafts raise them above the water so they can move swiftly over the surface with very little friction.

Some engineers have even proposed using magnetic fields to make mass transit vehicles float frictionlessly a fraction of an inch above their guiding rails.

Charles Lindbergh, the first man to make a solo airplane flight over the Atlantic Ocean, is reported to have said, following a roller coaster ride on the Coney Island Cyclone, "A ride on the Cyclone is a greater thrill than flying an airplane at top speed."

LOOP-THE-LOOP ROLLER COASTER

One of the greatest thrills at an amusement park is a ride on the roller coaster. Many roller coasters include not only steep inclines and sharp turns but one or more 360° loops as well. How can the cars stay on the tracks when they are upside down?

Some might answer that the cars have wheels beneath as well as above the tracks. This is true. But it's not the answer, because you might ask, "Why don't people fall out of the cars when they are upside down?"

When anything moves in a circle, it has an acceleration (change in velocity) toward the center of the circle. This may seem strange to you but you can prove it for yourself. Take a pill bottle and fill it nearly full of warm water. Leave just one air bubble in the tube. Hold the tube horizontally and accelerate it (increase its speed) in a forward direction. You will see the bubble move in the direction of the acceleration which is always in the same direction as the force on the tube (*see diagram*). The tube is a miniature accelerometer.

Now that you are convinced that the bubble in your accelerometer moves in the same direction as the acceleration, tape your accelerometer to a turntable or take it with you on a merry-go-round ride. You will see the bubble move toward the center of the circular path it follows (*see diagram*).

When something falls, gravity makes it go faster and faster as it approaches the ground. Its speed increases thirty-two feet per second (ten meters per second) every second it falls. After one second, it will be going thirty-two feet per second (or twenty-two miles per hour); after two seconds, its speed will be sixty-four feet per second (forty-four miles per hour); its speed will be ninety-six feet per second after three seconds, and so on. If you *stand* at the top of a loop in a roller coaster track and drop a penny, it will fall with an acceleration of thirty-two feet per second every

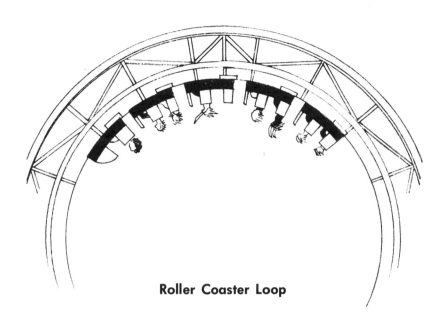

Roller Coaster Loop

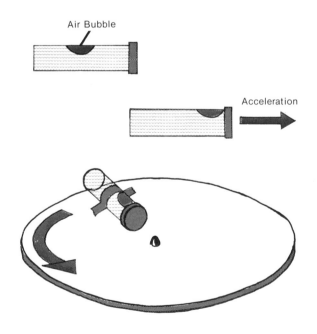

Air Bubble

Acceleration

An Accelerometer

second. But if you are *riding* in a moving upside-down roller coaster car at the top of the same loop, the penny will not fall from your hand.

The roller coaster cars and the people in them are all being accelerated toward the center of the loop. The acceleration is, of course, downward, since that's where the center of the loop is located. If the downward acceleration of the looping roller coaster car is greater than the acceleration due to gravity, then nothing can fall out of the car. Everything is already accelerating downward at a rate greater than thirty-two feet per second every second.

Suppose the cars are moving at a speed of only forty feet per second (twenty-seven miles per hour) at the top of a loop that has a diameter of fifty feet. The acceleration toward the center of the loop will be sixty-four

Water That Doesn't Fall

feet per second every second. The cars and everything in them are being pushed down twice as hard by the tracks as by gravity. If you are riding in one of the cars, you'll feel the seat pushing you downward. If you drop the penny at the top of the loop, it will move toward the floor of the car because the car is accelerating downward faster than the free-falling penny. In fact, you will not fall from the car at the top of the loop unless it is moving along the fifty-foot loop at a speed slower than twenty-eight feet per second (nineteen miles per hour).

To see how this works, you can make a model roller coaster loop of your own from flexible toy racing-car track or put some water in a pail and swing it in a vertical circle (*see diagram*). Not a drop of water will fall from the pail. How slowly can you swing the pail before water falls out at the top of the circle?

At Fenway Park in Boston men still scurry along planks, dropping numbered boards into the proper slots on the scoreboard. The same procedure was followed in most other ball parks twenty years ago, but today most stadiums have introduced elaborate electronic scoreboards to entertain and excite, as well as inform, the fans.

SCOREBOARDS

The first scoreboard gimmick to delight the fans was developed in Columbia, South Carolina, where a toy goose was moved along the top of the scoreboard to drop a "goose egg" into the proper "nest" when the opponents failed to score in their half of the inning. But the first elaborate major league scoreboard was developed at Chicago under the direction of Bill Veeck in 1960.

Veeck was with the Chicago Cubs in 1940, when he saw a pinball machine light up like a volcano in the stage play *The Time of Your Life.* He never forgot the event, and in 1960, the White Sox organization which he directed invested $350,000 in a "wild" scoreboard. Whenever a White Sox player hit a home run, the person operating the scoreboard would turn on switches that set off fireworks, flashing lights, sirens, and a loudspeaker system that amplified a recording of a choir singing "Hallelujah."

The electronic scoreboards in stadiums today cost three to ten times as much as Veeck's original innovation. The astroboard in Houston's Astrodome is four stories high and a city block long. It contains 50,000 light bulbs and 12,000 miles of wiring.

The patterns seen on scoreboards, be they numbers, words, or pictures, are painted with lights. By turning some lights on and leaving others off, an enormous variety of scores, messages, cartoons, and even portraits, can be displayed. By turning some lights on as others go off, it is possible to produce animation on the screen. A "bouncing ball" can be made to move from word to word or through the legs of a cartoon infielder who lowers his glove too late.

Instead of a hundred men rushing along planks behind the scoreboard to turn lights on and off, the scoreboard is operated by one or two people seated at a console. By pressing a button, he or she is able to activate any

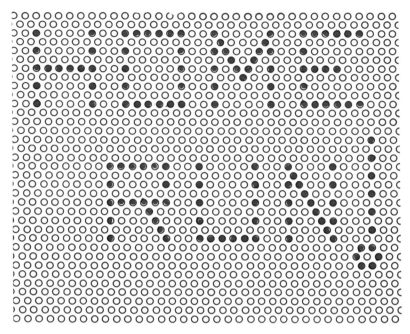

Scoreboard

one of a number of computerized programs that have been placed on tape and stored in a computer.

Next time you go to a ball park or a coliseum, watch the scoreboard carefully to see the lights go on and off to produce a variety of patterns. If you wonder how teams can afford such elaborate and expensive scoreboards, pull out your ticket stub and look at the price.

Many uninformed people spend a lot of time trying to invent perpetual motion machines: machines that will run forever without fuel. Scientists and engineers know that such a device cannot be built. But have they ever watched a dipping bird drink?

DIPPING BIRD

You can lead a dipping bird to water but you can't make it drink unless you first wet its felt-covered head. Once you have done that, the bird will begin dipping. It will even dip if there is no water to "drink." If you give the bird a glass of water into which it can dip its long felt-covered beak, it will go on "drinking" for days. But why does it continue to dip and drink hour after hour?

Watch the bird carefully after you wet its head. You will see colored liquid moving up the long straight glass tube. It moves from the lower bulb to the bird's head. The head is really another glass bulb that has been covered with felt.

Notice that in the beginning the bird's body is tilted slightly forward. As the liquid moves from the lower to the upper bulb, some of the bird's weight must shift from its lower body to its head. This causes the bird to tip forward in much the same way that a seesaw will move if the person on one end moves closer to or farther from the center of the board.

But why does the liquid move up the tube? You'll find a clue to answering this question if you fan a dipping bird. Its drinking rate will soon increase; that is, it will drink more often.

As you probably know, water evaporates faster when there is a breeze. On a windy day puddles disappear quickly, and clothes dry fast. For the same reason, the water on a dipping bird's felt-covered head evaporates faster when you fan it.

If you've ever stepped out of a pool, lake, or ocean and stood in a breeze, you know that evaporation has a cooling effect. You might have started to shiver even though it was a warm day. This happens because the water as it evaporates absorbs heat. Everyone who has boiled water knows that it takes heat to change a liquid to a gas. Even if water changes to a gas (water vapor) at a temperature well below the boiling point, it still

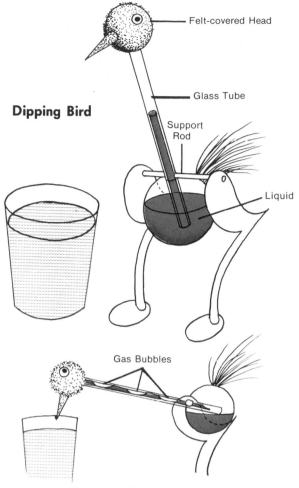

Dipping Bird

Felt-covered Head

Glass Tube

Support
Rod

Liquid

Gas Bubbles

Dipping Bird "Drinking"

requires a large amount of heat energy. This heat comes from your skin and so you feel cold.

The liquid inside a dipping bird is usually ether or another liquid that has a low boiling point and is easily changed from liquid to gas or gas to liquid. As water evaporates from the bird's head, the gas in the upper bulb is cooled. Some of the gas condenses to a liquid as it cools, and the pressure of the gas in the upper bulb decreases. The pressure of the gas above the liquid in the lower bulb is now greater than the pressure of the gas in the upper bulb. Therefore, liquid is pushed up the tube.

To check up on this idea, you can increase the pressure of the gas in the lower bulb and see what happens. Simply hold the lower bulb in your hand. Heat from your hand will warm the gas and increase the pressure. Again, you will see the liquid rise up the tube. This will happen even if the bird's head is completely dry.

After the bird has tipped forward to take a drink, the lower end of the long tube is no longer submerged in the liquid. Bubbles of gas move up the tube to equalize the pressure. With no difference in pressure, gravity causes the liquid to fall back into the lower bulb. As the weight shifts back to its lower body, the bird returns to its normal position and the cycle begins again.

Do you see why a dipping bird is *not* a perpetual motion machine? If you don't, think about what will happen when there is no water left for the bird to drink.

IN THE FUTURE

The solar energy that strikes the earth every hour is more than enough to meet the world's power needs for a year. There is plenty of energy available from the sun, but capturing and using this energy present problems that we are just beginning to solve.

SOLAR HEATER

The earth is running out of oil, but the sun has over a billion years' supply of fuel. This is why you may have seen some large glass-covered "boxes" on the roofs of houses in your community. These are called solar collectors. They convert the sun's energy into heat that can be used to keep houses warm and to supply hot water for washes, baths, and showers.

The basic parts of a solar heating system are 1) a collector, 2) a fluid to transfer heat, 3) a way to store heat for sunless days and nights.

The most common collector is a flat metal plate that is painted black. A copper tube filled with water winds within the plate as shown in the diagram. Insulation behind the plate reduces heat losses, while a double layer of glass covers the collector's face.

Sunlight passes through the glass cover to the black plate where it is absorbed and converted to heat. Some infrared radiation is produced by the hot black plate, but it cannot pass through the glass. Thus, the glass plates not only let energy into the collector, they prevent most of the energy radiated by the collector from escaping. This ability of glass to allow visible but not infrared light to be transmitted is called the greenhouse effect. It explains why greenhouses are so warm on sunny winter days.

The collectors are tilted so that sunlight falls directly on the black surface. If the winter sun is only 30°–40° above the horizon, collectors in the northern hemisphere should face south and be tilted 50°–60° to be perpendicular to the sun's rays.

Water is the most common fluid used to transfer heat from the collectors into the building. In some systems air is used. The collectors for air

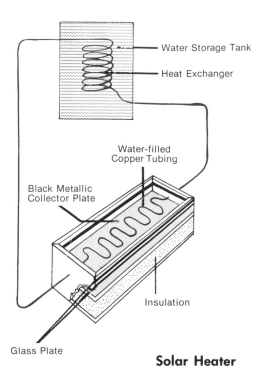

Water Storage Tank

Heat Exchanger

Water-filled
Copper Tubing

Black Metallic
Collector Plate

Insulation

Glass Plate

Solar Heater

transfer systems consist of black sheet-metal ducts about one inch deep and two feet wide. In either kind of system the warm fluid rises and flows into the building where the heat is stored and used.

Without sunlight the solar collector does not work, so there must be some way to store heat for nights and cloudy days. If air is used to transfer heat, large quantities of crushed rock can absorb and store heat from the circulating air. The stones are usually kept in a basement and are surrounded by insulation. Water systems store heat in large tanks of water. Since water can absorb more heat than an equal volume of stone, the water tanks need not be as large as the rock bins.

Most solar heating systems are not capable of supplying all the heat needed for very cold periods when there is little or no sunlight for several days. A backup system that uses oil, gas, or electricity is common.

Solar heat is expensive but the method is still in its infancy. Engineers and inventors are studying better ways to use, collect, and store the sun's energy. Certain coatings applied to the collectors improve their ability to absorb solar radiation. An evacuated space above the collector eliminates

106

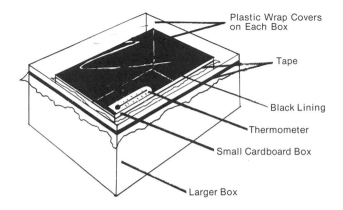

Plastic Wrap Covers
on Each Box

Tape

Black Lining

Thermometer

Small Cardboard Box

Larger Box

Model of a Solar Heater

any heat losses due to conduction or convection. Lenses and mirrors can be used to increase the amount of sunlight falling on a collector. It may also be possible to store heat in materials such as Glauber's salt. These substances release large amounts of heat when they change from a liquid to a solid.

These and other modifications of solar heating systems are being investigated. You can do your own "research" by building two of the simple solar heaters shown in the diagram. Tip one box so its face is perpendicular to the sun's rays while the other lies flat on the ground. Compare the temperature changes in the two boxes. Line one box with aluminum foil instead of black paper, and compare temperature changes. Use but a single layer of plastic wrap on one box. Try a Styrofoam box instead of cardboard. Measure the rate of temperature change at noon, early morning, and late afternoon. What other experiments can you think of to try?

Despite the present high cost of installing a solar heating system, the rising price of oil makes solar heating economical over a period of several years. After all, the fuel used for solar heating is free and almost unlimited.

In power plants, electricity is produced by turning a turbine connected to an electric generator. Sometimes the turbine is rotated by water rushing through a dam. More often, steam under high pressure is directed against the blades of the turbine. The steam is produced by heating water, usually with burning oil or coal. But there is another way to heat the water. We can use atomic energy generated in nuclear reactors.

NUCLEAR REACTORS

As fossil fuels (oil and coal) become increasingly scarce, nuclear (atomic) reactors provide an alternative method for producing electric power.

The core of such a reactor usually consists of the uranium or plutonium fuel encased in metal rods. These fuel elements are surrounded by water which serves to transfer heat and moderate the reaction.

A uranium atom, like the atoms of all elements, has at its center a tiny dense nucleus that contains protons and neutrons. These two kinds of particles have just about the same mass, but neutrons have no electric charge, while protons each carry one unit of positive charge.

All uranium atoms have 92 protons in their nuclei, but they differ in the number of neutrons they possess. These different kinds of uranium atoms are called isotopes. One isotope, uranium 235, has 143 neutrons in addition to the 92 protons (143 + 92 = 235). This particular isotope may *fission* (split) when its nuclei are struck by slow-moving neutrons. The nucleus absorbs a neutron and then breaks up into lighter particles such as barium and krypton nuclei as well as several free neutrons. If enough uranium 235 nuclei are present, the neutrons released by one fissioned atom can cause other nuclei to split.

The free neutrons released during fission are moving too fast to be absorbed by uranium 235 nuclei. If these neutrons are to be used to produce additional fissions, their speed must be reduced (moderated). Collisions between the neutrons and the water that fills the core of the reactor decrease the speed of the neutrons to a point where they can be absorbed by other uranium nuclei.

If we could weigh the smaller nuclei of such atoms as barium and

108

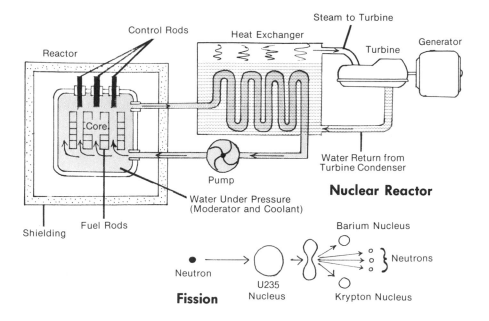

Nuclear Reactor

Fission

krypton as well as the neutrons released after an atom fissions, we would find them to weigh less than the original uranium nucleus. The missing material is converted to energy. The amount of energy released is equal to the mass loss times the speed of light squared. This can be summarized by the now famous equation: $E = mc^2$. Because the speed of light is so large (300,000 km/sec or 186,000 mi/sec) a small loss of material results in enormous quantities of energy.

The heat energy released in a reactor is absorbed by the water that surrounds the core and carried to the heat exchanger. There heat is transferred to the cooler water from the turbine to produce steam. As you can see in the diagram, the water that circulates through the reactor is entirely separate from the water and steam that flow through the turbine. The water that cools the reactor remains a liquid even though its temperature is well above 100°C (212°F) because it is under very high pressure.

To regulate the rate of the reaction in the core, boron steel control rods may be lowered or raised as necessary. These rods absorb neutrons and, therefore, reduce the fission rate when they are lowered into the core. By properly adjusting these rods, the rate can be regulated so that only one neutron per fission is available to fission another atom of uranium. In this way a constant rate of reaction and heat production is assured.

Because the fission products such as barium and krypton are very radioactive, the reactor must be shielded. The shielding is usually a thick wall of concrete that prevents the passage of gamma rays and other harmful radiation.

While nuclear reactors serve as an alternate source of power, many people oppose this form of energy. They fear that accidents within the plant, such as the one at Three Mile Island in Pennsylvania, or during the shipment of waste products that must be periodically removed from the core present a danger to which the public should not be subjected. It is true that accidents and the shipment and storage of nuclear wastes present the possibility of the release of dangerous radioactive material. On the other hand, the rising costs of oil and its decreasing abundance make it necessary to find and use other sources of energy. At the present time, solar energy and the energy available from fusion reactions are not at a stage where they can be used to generate large amounts of electrical energy. Coal is a possible energy source that might be used for as long as a century, but it is a prolific source of air pollution as well. You might like to investigate both sides of this question and draw your own conclusions.

As you can see, the problem is not an easy one to solve. It will require considerable research and compromise over the next few years.

J. K. Starley, an Englishman, probably built the first electric car in 1888. Between 1900 and 1912, over one hundred companies manufactured electric cars. Electric cars were on the roads and electric trolley lines ran throughout and between cities. After 1930, electric cars were seldom seen. They were slower than gasoline-powered cars; early twentieth-century America was a rural country and there was often no electricity to charge batteries on farms and in country towns; gasoline became inexpensive and so did gasoline-powered cars after Henry Ford began to mass produce the Model T; electric starters eliminated the need to crank gasoline engines; and electric cars could not go far without stopping to charge the batteries.

ELECTRIC CARS

Today, gasoline is expensive and oil supplies are becoming limited, but most people still drive cars with gasoline engines. Gasoline engines pollute our atmosphere, while electricity is now available throughout the country. Perhaps this is the time to go back to non-polluting, quiet, electric cars.

Electric cars, like golf carts, are powered by batteries stored in the car. When you hear the word "battery," you probably think of the lead-acid batteries found in most cars today. But there are other kinds of batteries. Silver-zinc batteries, for instance, can deliver about five times as much energy per pound as lead-acid batteries. Unfortunately, they cost about ten times as much. The batteries in electric cars will have to be recharged every 100 miles or so. Silver-zinc cells can only be recharged about 300 times, but lead-acid batteries can go through 400 operating cycles. Silver-cadmium batteries can be recharged 3,000 times, but they cost as much as silver-zinc batteries. Since an electric car will need sixty to one hundred and fifty batteries, the cost of the silver batteries alone for one car would be over $15,000; lead-acid batteries would cost about $1,500.

The batteries supply current to an electric motor or motors that will, through belts or gears, turn the electric car's wheels (*see diagram*).

A set of automatic controls will probably be developed to control the switching and regulating that will be necessary to operate the car efficiently

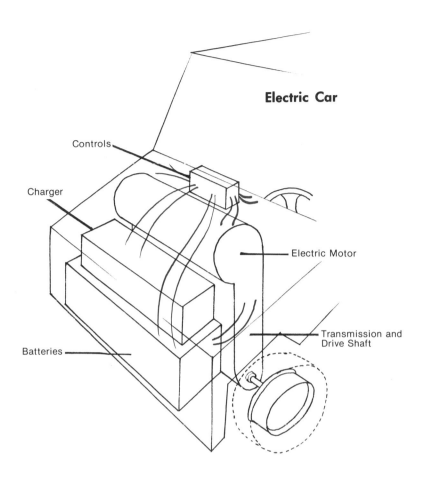

Electric Car

Controls

Charger

Electric Motor

Transmission and
Drive Shaft

Batteries

and effectively. Direct-current electricity will sometimes be changed to alternating current or pulses of direct current. Voltages will be varied by switching batteries from series to parallel; large and small currents will be turned on and off or be converted from one to the other over short periods of time. By a series of automatic electronic feedback systems, the controls will vary the electrical output to meet the requirements of the car at any particular moment.

When the car is going down hill, the motor can be used as a generator to charge the batteries. As the motion energy (kinetic energy) of the car is used to generate electricity, it will have a braking effect on the car since the moving wheels will be used to turn the generator or generators.

To overcome the delay and inconvenience of waiting for the car's batteries to be recharged periodically, you may be able to drive your electric car into an "electric station" and say, "A new set of batteries, please." The attendant will remove your tray of batteries and insert a new set that has been recently charged. You will pay a service or rental charge and drive away.

It is true that quiet electric cars are more efficient than today's popular gasoline-driven automobiles. Unfortunately, they have a short range (100 miles or so) between battery recharges, are slower, and are currently very expensive. Extensive research may increase the range and speed of these cars while reducing their cost. But have you considered what would happen if we suddenly replaced all the internal combustion engines in our cars with electric motors and batteries?

To charge these batteries, we would have to build many more expensive electric power plants. And where do power plants get their energy? From oil and coal mostly. The pollution from automobiles would be nearly zero, but the increased pollution from coal- and oil-burning power plants would be much greater. But, you say, "Electric cars are much more efficient so there *would* be less pollution."

It's true that electric cars have an efficiency of about 56 percent while gasoline cars are only about 25 percent efficient. However, power plants are only 40 percent efficient at best. We must take that into account when we consider the actual efficiency of the electric car. Forty percent of 56 percent is about 22 percent, so we would not eliminate pollution. There are other factors to consider, of course, but a switch to electric cars will not solve all our air pollution problems although it could make our cities and highways much less noisy.

A steam engine was used in the first automobile to travel faster than a train. It was a Stanley Steamer, which was clocked at 150 miles per hour in 1907.

Steam cars, like electric cars, could not compete with the gasoline-fueled internal-combustion engines. People were afraid to drive a vehicle that had an open flame and hot steam. In the winter huge clouds of white vapor were produced when the car was running, and the water used to make the steam froze when the car was not in use. In addition, it took about fifteen minutes to get up steam and frequent stops were necessary to replace the water lost through boiling.

STEAM CAR

Steam cars are rarely seen today, but a number of companies are investigating them and building experimental models.

The heat to produce steam comes from the external combustion of gasoline, kerosene, fuel oil, or most any combustible fluid. The working fluid is water or perhaps an organic liquid such as thiophene or Freon (*see diagram*).

Water normally boils at 100°C (212°F), but the pressure within the closed system will raise the steam temperatures and the boiling point to three or four times the normal boiling temperature.

Steam from the generator will enter the cylinders through valves and drive pistons downward in the same way that exploding gases move the piston in a gasoline engine. As the steam expands into the cylinder it will, like all gases, cool.

The pistons are attached to a crankshaft, and as one piston is forced downward by incoming steam, another is moving upward to expel the cooler steam through an exhaust valve.

Steam from the exhaust valve goes to a condenser, where it is cooled by moving air. The liquid is then pumped back into the generator, where it is heated and converted back to steam again.

A conventional transmission, fly wheel, driveshaft, and differential will transfer the motion of the crankshaft to the axles and wheels.

Because the system is closed and the condensed steam returned to the

Steam Car

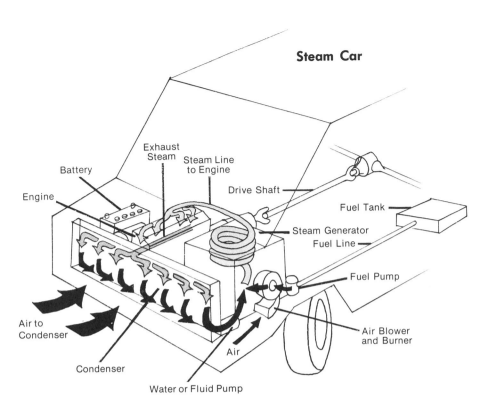

Exhaust Steam

Battery

Steam Line to Engine

Engine

Drive Shaft

Fuel Tank

Steam Generator

Fuel Line

Fuel Pump

Air to Condenser

Air Blower and Burner

Condenser

Air

Water or Fluid Pump

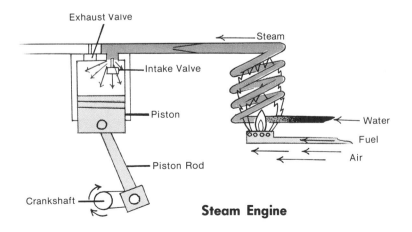

Exhaust Valve

Steam

Intake Valve

Piston

Water

Fuel

Air

Piston Rod

Crankshaft

Steam Engine

boiler, the white clouds of vapor that swirled about the Stanley Steamer will not be found around modern steam cars if they become popular. Fifteen seconds, not fifteen minutes, is the warm-up time required before steam can move the car. The problem of freezing in cold weather remains unless an organic fluid with a low freezing temperature is used. The miles per gallon of fuel figures are about the same as those for gasoline-powered cars.

The major advantage of steam cars is that the fuel is burned externally. Plenty of oxygen reaches the fuel, and so it burns almost completely. Very little carbon monoxide, oxides of nitrogen, and other polluting gases are produced. In fact, the steam engine produces only about 1 percent as much air pollution as the internal-combustion engine (ICE).

Will a modern Stanley Steamer replace today's internal-combustion engine? Not likely! Better emission-control exhaust systems will probably be added to the ICE instead, at least as long as oil reserves provide gasoline. Beyond that, who knows? Perhaps burning hydrogen will some-day provide the fuel to heat steam generators in cars throughout the world.

*On April 12, 1961, Yuri Gagarin became the first human
to orbit the earth in space (above the atmosphere). Since
July 20, 1969, when American astronauts Neil Armstrong
and Buzz Aldrin walked on the moon's surface, the idea
of colonizing space became not a dream but a matter of
time, research, and money.*

SPACE SHUTTLE

Prior to the Space Shuttle, the rockets used to launch satellites and spaceships were not used again, nor were the vehicles that carried men and materials into space employed a second time. The economics of building spacelabs required that the ships used for transportation be used many times. We simply cannot afford the luxury of "one shot" spaceships.

The Space Shuttle consists of three parts: the Orbiter; an external tank (ET) that carries fuel for the Orbiter's three main engines; and a pair of solid-fuel rocket boosters (SRB), one on each side of the external tank (*see diagram*).

At lift-off, the SRB's and the Orbiter's main engines fire in parallel to supply the force needed to carry the vehicle to an altitude of 27 miles (43 kilometers) and a speed of 3,200 miles (5,100 kilometers) per hour, just 126 seconds after blast-off. There the SRBs separate from the ET and parachute into the Atlantic Ocean about 150 miles (240 kilometers) downrange from the Kennedy Space Center. The 149-foot-long SRBs float until a tugboat arrives to tow them back to port so they can be prepared for the next voyage.

The Orbiter engines continue to drive the ship and ET upward to an altitude of 66 miles (106 kilometers) and a speed of 17,500 miles per hour (28,000 kilometers per hour). At this point all the liquid hydrogen and oxygen have been used up so the tank (ET) is jettisoned. The huge tank (154 by 28½ feet) burns up as it re-enters the atmosphere.

The fuel needed beyond this position is relatively small. The rockets that make up the orbital maneuvering system are used to bring the Orbiter into a stable orbit anywhere from 110 to 700 miles (180–1,100 kilometers) from the earth's surface.

The Orbiter's speed (slightly greater than 17,500 miles per hour) in orbit, together with its average rate of fall toward the earth due to gravity,

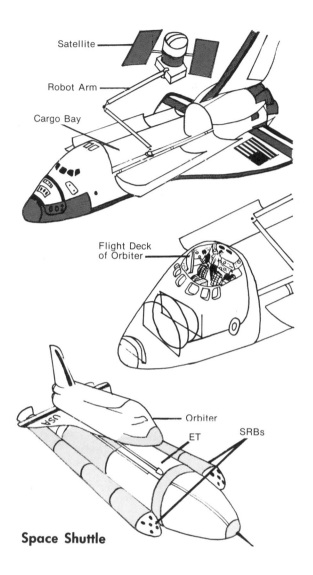

Satellite

Robot Arm

Cargo Bay

Flight Deck
of Orbiter

Orbiter

ET

SRBs

Space Shuttle

causes it to move along a curved path that matches the curvature of the earth. Consequently, the Orbiter, or any other satellite, will remain in orbit at such a speed.

The forty-four small rockets placed about the ship, together with two small rear-rocket engines comprise the orbital maneuvering system (OMS). The OMS is used to move the Orbiter from one orbit to another, to rendezvous with spacelabs or satellites, and to turn the ship for positioning during payload deliveries and re-entry.

118

Each Shuttle mission can deliver a 65,000-pound (29,500-kilogram) payload of equipment, materials, food, oxygen, etc., in its 60-by-15-foot cargo bay. The missions will service satellites or spacelabs, carry new satellites and spacelabs into precise orbits, retrieve payloads from orbit for reuse or study, and allow scientists on board to carry out experimental work.

The cargo bay contains a long robot arm that is used to manipulate satellites, spacelab modules, and other objects that are being moved out of or into the Orbiter. Up to 32,000 pounds (14,500 kilograms) can be stored in the cargo space for the return trip to earth.

Once the mission is accomplished, which may take anywhere from a week to a month, one or more of the rockets in the OMS will be fired in the direction of the Orbiter's path in order to reduce its speed. At a slower speed, its path becomes sharper than the earth's curvature and it will begin its journey back to earth.

Upon re-entering the earth's atmosphere, it will rapidly slow down as it rubs against the air. The heat produced by the friction between the air and the spacecraft will create temperatures as high as 1,300°C (2,300°F). This would ignite the Orbiter and it would burn like a meteor (shooting star) were it not for the silica coated ceramic blocks that cover its fuselage. These blocks rapidly radiate heat to prevent burning.

After Orbiter has passed through most of the atmosphere, its speed will be normal for an ordinary aircraft. It will glide to a "dead stick" landing on the special three-mile landing strip at Cape Canaveral.

After two weeks for inspection, repair, and reloading, it will be ready for another trip to space.

The Space Shuttle has reduced the cost of putting payloads into orbit from $1,000 per pound to under $200 per pound. Some people estimate that future changes in the system will reduce the price to as little as $25 per pound. If the cost of sending materials into space can be reduced this much, the creation of space colonies becomes a real possibility. We may one day mine minerals on the moon, manufacture ball bearings in space, and operate an orbiting solar power plant beaming microwaves to earth where they will be converted, pollution-free, into electricity.

INDEX

(Page numbers in italics indicate an illustration of the subject mentioned)

ROBERT GARDNER is head of the science department at Salisbury School, Salisbury, Connecticut, where he teaches physics, chemistry, and physical science. He has written several science books for children and numerous articles for *Nature and Science, The Science Teacher, The Biology Teacher, Science and Children, The Physics Teacher,* and *Current Science.* He is the author and coauthor of several books for Doubleday, some of which are *Shadow Science, Magic Through Science, Moving Right Along* and *Basic Lacrosse Strategy.*

JEFFREY BROWN received his B.E.A. degree in graphic design from the Maryland Institute, College of Art. He studied art education at Kean College in New Jersey, and received his M.A.Ed. degree from the Hartford Art School of the University of Hartford. His work has been exhibited at the University of Hartford, the Fell's Point Gallery in Baltimore, and galleries in Northwest Connecticut. Mr. Brown is presently teaching studio art, art history, film, and photography at the Salisbury School in Salisbury, Connecticut.